SPARE
the
ROD

Phil E. Quinn

SPARE the ROD

Breaking The Cycle of Child Abuse

Abingdon Press

Nashville

SPARE THE ROD
Breaking the Cycle of Child Abuse

This book is printed on acid-free paper.

Library of Congress Cataloging-in-Publication Data

QUINN, P.E.(Phil E.), 1950–
Spare the rod: breaking the cycle of child abuse/
Phil E. Quinn.   p.   cm.
1. Child abuse—United States—Prevention.
2. Child rearing—United States.   I. Title.
   HV741.Q575   1988   87-31825
   649'.64—dc 19   CIP

ISBN 0-687-39145-8 (alk. paper)

Scripture quotations are from the Revised Standard Version of the
Bible, copyrighted 1946, 1952, © 1971, 1973 by the Division of Christian
Education of the National Council of the Churches of Christ in the U.S.A.

MANUFACTURED BY THE PARTHENON PRESS AT
NASHVILLE, TENNESSEE, UNITED STATES OF AMERICA

This book is dedicated to the
Reverend W. Scott Root,
who helped me find the key to
unlock the prison of my childhood,
and to all those—young and old—who still remain
in bondage to an abusive childhood.

CONTENTS

ACKNOWLEDGMENTS

It has been said that any road will do for those who do not know where they are going. But not any road would have been adequate for the purpose of this book. Although I knew where I was going, I was not always so sure how to get there!

I could not have arrived at this destination without the support and guidance of some very special people. They became my eyes when I could not see His truth, my ears when I could not hear His voice, my heart when I could not feel His love and presence. They uplifted, inspired, challenged, and encouraged me. They were my guides in a world where it could have been so easy to become lost!

How I shall always treasure those moments of love and support given me by the Reverend Bill and Carol Dalglish as I struggled with some very threatening concepts! Without their faith in me, their insights, and their strength, it would have been so easy to abandon this work altogether.

And Laura Comer—what a gift she was! Her gentle challenges, warm smile, and endless sharing of ideas and feelings helped bring a spirit to this work that it would otherwise lack.

And what of Angie Sloan Powell and the many hours we spent talking on the phone and traveling from one speaking engagement to another? Her unselfish gift of time and self nourished me in times of greatest spiritual need.

And to my wife, Melissa, I offer special thanks for pushing me to be more than I thought possible.

PREFACE

You know me as Peter. You were first introduced to me in *Cry Out! Inside the Terrifying World of an Abused Child* (Abingdon Press, 1984). Through that book you were able to experience some of the pain and horror of child abuse. That was my purpose.

It is not enough that we know the problem exists in the lives of thousands of our children. Nor is it enough that we gather in groups and forums to discuss the problem. To stop child abuse and domestic violence in this country, we must act! But most of us will not be sufficiently motivated to do what must be done to prevent this senseless tragedy until our hearts and minds are united in a synthesis of understanding and compassion that will drive us to a personal commitment. For most of us, this will occur when the agony of our children becomes the agony of a nation crying out for mercy on behalf of all children everywhere. Only when their pain becomes our own will we be more inclined to utilize our resources to prevent child abuse than to pay for its inevitable consequences.

In *Cry Out!* you were able to share with me the pain of so

11

many children who watch their families torn apart by divorce, the grief that accompanies the loss of parents and siblings, the anxiety and confusion of moving from one foster home to another. I hope you came to understand why children who survive such an experience cannot realistically be expected to grow into healthy, well-adjusted young adults.

As a reader, you shared in the traumatic experience of my adoption into a family that, from all appearances, seemed ideal. You watched with a horror no less than my own as that family became abusive. You were able to experience vicariously several types of severe child abuse—physical beatings and torture, emotional assault and neglect, sexual abuse, and the systematic destruction of a developing child's self-image. That section was by far the most difficult for me to write and for you to read. It brought you intimately inside the world of an abused child.

Many of you responded with letters that pledged support for our work in the prevention of child abuse. Some of you have become involved in your own communities' efforts on behalf of abused children. And all of you are now aware of the life-threatening problem.

But to relate what it is like to be an abused child tells only half the story. The other half, which we dare not overlook, concerns what happens when abused children grow up; when they learn they can hit back! *Renegade Saint* (Abingdon Press, 1986), a companion to *Cry Out!* completes Peter's story; but more important, it describes the consequences of child abuse in the lives of the victims who survive.

It is my hope that those who read that volume come to realize how many of society's problems—delinquency, crime, rape, murder, prostitution, domestic violence—are rooted in childhoods characterized by abuse. Violence perpetuates violence. There is no greater truth that goes so profoundly unacknowledged.

The most painful part of writing *Renegade Saint* was sharing the fact that I, a victim of severe abuse, became an abusive parent. Although this is not an uncommon result, it was not easy to be so painfully honest. Failure to do so, however, would have denied that book its greatest message of hope: It *is* possible for victims, and even perpetrators, to break the cycle of abuse! The legacy of abuse does not need to be perpetual suffering. The cycle can be broken! I did it. Others can too—maybe not in the same way, for no two people are identical—but perhaps by making changes in the conditions that cause most child abuse. That is the purpose of this third book.

After reading the first two books, many people have expressed a frustration shared by countless others. You tell me that in *Cry Out!* I have clearly identified the problem and inspired you to become personally involved. In *Renegade Saint*, I helped you understand the consequences of severe abuse and provoked within you a greater empathy for its surviving victims. But that is not enough. You want to know how you can help!

It is the responsibility of those who identify problems to also suggest solutions. *Spare the Rod* addresses two issues that are critical to the prevention of child abuse in its various forms. Since most child abuse is rooted in ignorance and tradition, the first task is to identify several of the most dangerous cultural beliefs that foster violence in the family. Then comes the challenge—to act, to become personally involved in the solution to the problem, to

13

make a personal choice between the ways of violence and the ways of love.

Child abuse will continue as long as we remain aloof, silent, and uninformed, making no concerted attack upon its source; and destruction of precious human lives will continue until at last we concede the worthlessness of all human life. When children are abused, we all suffer!

INTRODUCTION

Our Mission

Most parents would not intentionally harm their children, but some would! And some parents unintentionally do great harm to their children. These facts are becoming agonizingly apparent as more public attention has been drawn to the way we raise our children.

The modern period of medical and social awareness of child abuse began in 1961 when a Denver pediatrician, Dr. C. Henry Kempe, became alarmed by the number of children who came into his care with injuries that could not be explained as having resulted from accidents. In a symposium conducted that same year by the American Academy of Pediatricians, Dr. Kempe coined the phrase battered-child syndrome to identify intentionally inflicted injuries. The conclusions of that symposium were published the following year in the *Journal of the American Medical Association*, and the symptoms of the battered-child syndrome were clearly identified.

With media and public attention drawn to the problem, a great wave of public sentiment inspired lawmakers to act, and by 1974, all states had passed some form of

15

child-protection legislation. When the National Center for the Prevention of Child Abuse was established in Washington, D.C., federal money was made available to develop and implement programs to study and treat the problem. Child Protective Services, a separate department within Human Services, was formed for that purpose.

With the passage of reporting laws, greater media exposure of extreme cases, and the availability of research statistics, the American public was shocked to learn that child abuse is not an isolated occurrence found only within lower socioeconomic classes or as a by-product of drug abuse, alcoholism, or mental illness. Today, shock and disbelief still tend to characterize public and professional response to the single most serious threat to the children of this country. The prevalence of child abuse was then, and continues to be, both shocking and overwhelming.

In response to this growing awareness, vast amounts of money and professional time and energy have been spent in a daily attempt to deal with the problem. The goals of contemporary efforts are to stop child abuse where it is presently occurring, provide treatment for the victims in an attempt to reverse some of the damage done to their young fragile lives, and treat the abusive parent(s) in the hope that the abuse will not recur. In addition, legal sanctions allow official intervention when necessary to save the life of a child and, in extreme cases, criminal action against the abusers.

In terms of taxpayers' dollars as well as human suffering, the cost of dealing with child abuse after it has occurred is staggering. Not only must we pay for the protection and treatment of victims and bear the cost of rehabilitation or incarceration of perpetrators, but we must continue to pay as abused children grow into young adults who vent their rage and hostility against a society that allowed their childhoods to be stolen from them.

It takes more money, time, effort, resources, and professional expertise to cope with the consequences of abuse than it would have required to prevent it in the first place. Prevention is the solution!

Legislation for the protection of our children is important. But it is not the final answer. Neither is raising taxes to pay for the consequences of abuse. Instead, we must turn our attention to the root of the problem, where it begins and is allowed to flourish.

To solve the problem we have created, we must look inward—at ourselves and the way we raise our children. For it is there, in our thoughts, feelings, and beliefs about parenting, that child abuse has its roots. We are the problem. But we are also the solution.

Defining Child Abuse

A legal definition of child abuse has, as its primary purpose, the setting of statutory restraints within which the state can and must intervene in instances of abuse, and the establishment of guidelines for how and when to do so. Its purpose is not to destroy a family by removing the children and prosecuting the parents. These are last-resort measures, used only in extreme cases when criminal charges must be filed because of gross damage to the child, the child's removal from the home being the only feasible way to prevent repeated abuse. Most professionals agree that the best interest of children is served when the home can be made safe and the children allowed to remain with their parents.

Such a definition, however, deals with the problem after the fact. It is intended to result in secondary prevention: to

17

make sure the abuse does not recur and to deal with its consequences. But more often than not, this is too late for the victim. The damage is already done.

Laws are not the answer. We cannot legislate "good parenting," to insure healthy and wholesome relationships between children and their parents. It is impossible to force parents to love their children, or to want them. A minimal standard of care that will allow children to survive—that is the purpose of the legal definition of child abuse.

Parents and other caregivers need a *preventive* definition, which has as its primary purpose the *prevention* of child abuse. To that end, our description is not intended to be punitive, judgmental, or accusatory. However, it must be inclusive, in that all harm done to a child, either by intent or by accident, inevitably results in physical, emotional, or mental consequences which may impair the child's health and development. The purpose of our description is to help us identify actual or potential deficiencies in the interaction between ourselves and our children—not as a way to instill guilt, feelings of failure, inadequacy, and shame or fear of prosecution—but to help us correct and avoid those deficiencies and be the best possible parents for our children.

Our preventive description of child abuse, then, is **any assault, whether verbal, sexual, or physical, or any deprivation of basic health and welfare necessities—regardless of severity, parental intention, or observable effects on the child.**

With such a description, we are attempting to *prevent* abuse by acknowledging and eliminating the dynamics that contribute to it. If we can identify those attitudes and practices which can potentially lead to abuse, it will be

18

easier for us to recognize them and control, limit, or eliminate them. Knowing a loaded gun is in the nightstand will help us avoid being accidentally shot. Similarly, it is a great deal easier to treat a temporary parental dislike for a child than to overcome a chronic and severe pattern of parental rejection that has evolved over a number of years and become habitual in the life-style of the family.

The description becomes more clear when we consider it from the perspective of physical abuse. The fundamental issue in defining child abuse is not *whether* pain and suffering should be inflicted upon children, but How much pain is too much? How much suffering can we allow before it becomes immoral, unethical, or illegal? How much hitting is too much? When there are broken bones? Bruises? Concussions? Somewhere along a continuum of violence, ranging from not hitting at all to beating a child to death, we must arbitrarily draw a line that distinguishes righteous violence, which "disciplines," from evil violence, which destroys. But where?

Contemporary society tends to believe that *some* hitting of children is good and acceptable as a parenting technique—but certainly not *all* hitting. The good hitting, we euphemistically call spanking. The bad hitting, we call child abuse. The dilemma, as always, is, Where does spanking end and beating begin? For too many parents, a spanking ends when bleeding begins. With such a broad definition of physical abuse, children can be subjected to an incredible amount of pain and suffering before our perception of parental prerogative changes to one of parental abuse.

It is a curious phenomenon in our culture—which prides itself on justice and equal protection for all—that this dilemma does not exist in any relationship other than that

19

between adults and children. The very people who are least capable of protecting themselves are the ones least protected under the law! A perfectly acceptable act of violence directed at a child is a criminal act when directed at an adult.

A preventive description of physical abuse of children includes *all* hitting, with no distinction between good and bad hitting, acceptable and unacceptable suffering, mild and extreme pain. Any hitting, by definition, would be considered harmful in our relationships with children, just as it is in adult relationships.

Telling a chronically abusive parent that spanking a child is a good thing to do is like telling an alcoholic that social drinking is perfectly harmless. The result could be tragic.

Our Mission

Every child deserves the opportunity to grow and develop into a healthy, well-adjusted adult. Much work has been done to protect our children from physical and sexual abuse, but their hearts and minds must be protected as well. No childhood is safe unless protected from *all* forms of abuse. Rarely do healthy children grow out of unhealthy childhoods!

Children do not need to be motivated and controlled with physical or emotional pain. It is possible to raise children without hurting them. Parents need to learn nonviolent and nonpunitive parenting techniques which relieve tension, resolve conflict, and minimize trauma within the family, rather than intensifying it. They need to develop within themselves the capacity to remember their own insecure and helpless childhoods.

And this is our mission. Maybe then our homes will once

again become havens of peace and love within a chaotic world; once again become the safe, fertile soil in which to nourish our children's development into responsible adults. We must once again become good and faithful stewards of what God has placed in our care.

It is my sincere hope that this book will help to relieve our suffering; will inspire our commitment to healthy child rearing; will encourage more caring; and will not in any way deny our humanity, but uplift it in celebration and the challenge to become more humane in our understanding, patience, and compassion toward children—all children everywhere.

Our purpose, our prayer, our mission is to bring hope to your child and mine—and the child within us as well as the child before us.

CHAPTER ONE

A Matter of Choice

"It's show time, Phil!" the producer of the show announced as she rushed into the guest waiting room with an air of nervous excitement. "Are you ready?"

Resisting the panic that stirred within me, I took a deep breath and glanced in the full-length mirror to make sure my hair was in place and my tie straight. The reflection in the mirror held my attention for a moment. It was not that I particularly liked what I saw. I knew the man behind that reflection all too well to be misled by appearances!

What held my attention was the contrast between the image I saw at that moment and the images so often reflected in the eyes of people who had looked at me as a child and as an adolescent. I was more comfortable with what I believed others thought of me than with what I saw in the mirror. They seemed more accurate. Or maybe it was that I trusted other people's judgments about me more than my own!

For whatever reason, the image in the mirror both frightened and excited me. I was excited by the changes that appeared to have taken place in my life over the past couple of years, but I feared they were temporary and superficial. Was it the man who had changed, or just his image?

Who would have thought that I—a survivor of severe child abuse, a former biker, a socially maladjusted misfit, an unwanted wrinkle in the cosmic order—at the age of thirty-four would find myself standing in a major television studio, wearing a three-piece suit, shoes polished to a glossy shine, clean shaven and every hair in place, waiting to be a guest on a highly rated television talk show?

I felt inadequate and out of place. I did not belong here! I was an alien in a strange world that really had no place for me. My place was on the street, lost in the crowd of other victims, mute and alone, who survive in silent desperation as they remain trapped in the prison of an abusive childhood.

But here I was, only minutes away from lights, action, camera. How had it happened? Why was I here, trying to be something I was not? My greatest fear was that someone would look too closely and discover the real me, the me that was bad and unworthy of love and deserving of punishment. What would these good people think? Even more important, why would anyone listen to me?

At that moment, as I struggled with the same self-defeating thoughts that had paralyzed my childhood and set me up to fail as an adult, the words of Father Paul came slowly back to me. I had gone to see him to tell him of my appearance on the show. During the conversation, I had expressed my feelings of self-doubt.

"How can I possibly do what they have asked me to do?" I worried. "Maybe I shouldn't even go. I don't know what to say or even how to say it!"

23

"*You* can't do it!" Father Paul exclaimed passionately. "But God can! Why don't you just turn loose and let God use your mind and voice to speak his truth? Don't you trust him?"

"Trust God?" Father Paul's question stunned me. "I'm not sure I know what it means to trust anyone!"

"That's OK. God has called you to a very special purpose. He will provide you with all you need to accomplish that purpose. With God, you cannot fail!"

"But how will I know what to say to all those people?" I moaned.

"You are thinking too much about yourself!" Father Paul pointed out bluntly. "You're so busy complaining about what you do not have, you can't see what you do have! Don't you understand that with God, you have everything?"

It was then that he told me about Moses. God had instructed him to go before Pharaoh, ruler of all Egypt, to demand the release of the enslaved Hebrew people. Of all the people God could have chosen, Moses was probably the one who had most to lose by returning to the house of Pharaoh, where he had been raised.

After killing a palace guard for beating a Hebrew slave, Moses had been exiled from Egypt with a stern warning never to return. And yet God was adamant. It was Moses God wanted for this mission.

Moses, too, had complained of being inadequate to fulfill the task. Like me, he was not a public speaker. What could he say to the people? And why should they listen? How was he to win their support when bondage had become their way of life? Even more frightening, how was he—an outlaw in Pharaoh's court—to convince that mighty emperor to submit to the will of a God he could not even see?

The more Father Paul talked about Moses, the more I could identify with the man! In the months and years ahead, Moses would become an important role model for me as I pursued the ministry of child-abuse prevention. But at that moment, the only real kinship I could feel with Moses was the realization that I could no more resist God's call than could he!

"God will give you the words, Phil, if you will but empty your mind of doubt and fill it instead with his purpose. Just as he spoke to Pharaoh through the mouth of Moses, so will God empower you with all you need to speak his truth on that show!"

Father Paul's face was ablaze with the assurance of someone well acquainted with the power of God. I could not help trusting that what he said was the truth. Besides, when had I ever known him to be wrong?

"Turn loose and let God," he had said. Again and again those words spoke their message to my troubled mind as I stared at the unfamiliar figure in the mirror. It was incredible that one man could reflect such opposite images!

"Phil, it's time!" The woman pulled lightly on my arm. "Are you ready?"

"Yes! Yes, I'm ready," I answered with a calmness I could not explain. The panic was gone. In its place was a wonderful sense of peace, with just enough anxiety to keep me alert.

I gasped as the press of applause seemed to smother me like a heavy fog when we entered the studio. There must have been two hundred people in the audience!

I felt dizzy and a little weak in the knees as I followed the producer to the platform in front of several huge cameras. I could feel the curious and measuring stares of many pairs of eyes as I took the seat on the right; I was too self-conscious to look at the faces. She ran a small microphone up under my vest and clipped it to my tie, making sure as little wire as possible was exposed.

"How do you feel?" she asked in an intimate whisper as she made the final adjustment of my tie.

"Scared!" I whispered back.

"You'll do fine!" she reassured me softly. "Just relax and enjoy the show. You'll like the host. He's very good. You'll see!"

"Two minutes!" came a voice from somewhere beyond the lights.

There was a rush as the man I had heard so much about entered the studio and took his seat opposite me on the platform. He introduced himself with a warm smile and adjusted his microphone. Reaching across the table that separated us, he offered me his hand.

"Welcome to the show. I've read your book and have been looking forward to meeting you!"

"One minute!" boomed the voice. A hush fell over the audience as the cameras moved into final position for their opening shots.

"Thirty seconds!"

"What am I doing here?" screamed a voice deep inside me. Just a few seconds away from talking to a national television audience, I was scared to death. What if I could not remember what I wanted to say? What if I forgot the statistics? What if I did not know the answers to their questions? What if they did not believe me? What if . . . ? Suddenly I felt overwhelmed again. I wanted to run and hide.

"Turn loose and let God!" Father Paul's voice echoed in my mind. "Remember why you are there."

The kids. They were why I was sitting on a raised platform in front of a live audience and hot lights and television cameras. *The kids*—the thousands of nameless, faceless children, who at that very moment were being physically, emotionally, and sexually abused. I was there to cry out for mercy and compassion on their behalf, with the hope of inspiring viewers to become involved in stopping and preventing child abuse.

"Ten seconds! Nine. Eight. Seven. Six. Five. . . . "

"Please, dear God, don't let me fail!" I prayed silently as the final seconds ticked away.

"Three. Two. One."

After a few seconds of thunderous audience applause, the floor director signaled the host of the show as he sat poised and ready in front of one of the cameras.

"It is estimated that one million American children will be physically or sexually abused this year. Two thousand of those children will die. Clearly, the abuse of children is a very serious problem—a problem that deserves our attention. We will be discussing this national problem with a uniquely qualified expert on this show. In his book, *Cry Out!* he prefers to call himself Peter. We are going to find out why. Our guest is a survivor of severe child abuse himself. Stay with us as we explore the terrifying world of an abused child!"

He concluded his introduction with an inviting smile at the camera. On cue, the audience applause erupted. I watched the man visibly relax as the red light on the camera suddenly went dark. He told me there would be a three-minute break before the show resumed. Busy with questions from the stage crew, he left me to my own thoughts during the time-out.

"Thirty seconds!" came that voice again.

"OK, Phil, you ready?" the host asked casually as he settled more comfortably into his chair. This time he faced me rather than the camera.

"I think so!"

The final ten-second countdown began.

"Go!" The floor director pointed at us.

"We're talking about a very sensitive and painful subject this morning, with a man who has survived it. We're talking about child abuse. Welcome to the show, Peter!" He smiled as he spoke to me.

"Thank you. It means a lot to me to be here," I heard myself say.

"Peter is not your real name, is it?" he asked.

"No, it isn't."

"Do you mind if I ask why you did not use your own name in the book?"

"No, I don't mind." I focused on his question. "I didn't want to use my own name because I was afraid it would detract from the purpose of the book. Who I am is not important. My name is not important. What *is* important is that thousands of children out there right now, in homes all across the world, are being physically, emotionally, and sexually abused. They are the ones who need our help and attention. There is nothing we can do to change what happened to me. But we can do a lot to change what is happening to them! But only if we can see them!"

The words poured from my mouth. I had no idea where they were coming from or what I would say next. They just came, one after another, each one adding meaning to the one before it. I was amazed!

Within seconds, I lost all thought of myself. I forgot to be frightened. I forgot to be nervous. I forgot to worry about

28

what people might think or whether they would believe me or whether they would listen. I even forgot to worry about failing! It was as though something had taken possession of me; as though someone else were speaking. They were not my words. Nothing seemed to matter but the urgent message that poured from me.

"Just what is the purpose of the book?" he asked, moving the conversation along. "What is it you are trying to do?"

"I am an advocate, working to stop and prevent child abuse!" I exclaimed without hesitation. "I wrote the book as a way to draw attention to those children who so desperately need our help."

"Do you really believe child abuse can be prevented?" he pressed on. "Even with all the attention it's getting now, it seems to be getting worse instead of better!"

"Yes! Yes, child abuse *can* be prevented! We must never allow ourselves to despair when it comes to our children. We are all they have in this world. Without our hope, they have nothing!" I was excited! I could not say enough fast enough.

"I believe that approximately 70 to 80 percent of child abuse is preventable. Nowhere is it written that we must abuse our children. If it is possible for adults to abuse children, then it is equally possible *not* to abuse them! God does not provide the possibility of one without the other. In most cases, it is a matter of choice! Unconscious, perhaps, but a choice nonetheless. It is a choice all parents must make many times each day!"

There was no hesitation before the next question. It followed logically from what had just been said.

"If so much child abuse is preventable, as you say, then how can it be done? What must we do? Even more important, what must *I* do ?"

29

What must I do? the man had asked.

A similar question was put to Jesus one day by a wealthy young man who was not thinking of others so much as of himself. He was asking what he must do to inherit eternal life.

Jesus told him to keep the Commandments. The righteous young man had done so from youth, careful to live his life in obedience to the Commandments. The Gospel of Mark (10:17-22) tells us that Jesus loved the rich young man, so he pointed out the one thing the young man lacked. He instructed him to go and sell all his possessions, give the money to the poor, and then come and follow him.

The response of the rich young man is a matter of history. It was so incredibly human! Mark tells us, "At that saying his countenance fell, and he went away sorrowful; for he had great possessions." Who among us cannot empathize? Who among us can blame him? And yet, who among us does not hear a similar challenge when we stand in the presence of our Lord? Maybe we are not being challenged to surrender our wealth. Perhaps the challenge that faces us is to give up our prejudices, our self-righteousness, our bigotry or selfishness. Or maybe our challenge is to surrender our hurtful traditions and ignorance.

I believe Jesus was challenging the young man in the same way God challenged Moses and has challenged me. What was it Moses feared most?—losing his life to Pharaoh's revenge. What was it the rich young man feared most?—losing his wealth. And what was it I feared most?—losing my mind by having to reexperience those awful childhood abuses! Each of us is controlled by the fear of losing what is most important to us at the time. And yet, God calls each of us to entrust what is most important to the care of others while we pursue his purpose in our lives! Though we do not know what became of the rich young man, we do know that Moses was not killed by Pharaoh and that I did not lose my mind!

The rich young man did not like what he heard. Instead of assuring him that obedience to the law was enough, Jesus questioned his values and way of life. He called the man to confront his greatest fear—to choose what would be Lord and master in his life.

What must we do to save ourselves? Clearly, we must value our relationship with God more than anything we possess. We must follow Jesus!

What must we do to save our children? The answer to that is just as simple, but no easier. We might not like the answer. It will call all serious followers of Jesus, and certainly all caring parents, into a confrontation with our values and beliefs about what it means to be a parent. It will challenge the way we think and feel about family life, the relationship we have with our children, even our relationship with God. It may even require personal sacrifice—the sacrifice of letting old beliefs and practices die so that our children might live!

This book will attempt to answer the question put to me on that television show several years ago. It is the same question many of you have been asking since my first book was published. What must we do—what must *I* do—to stop and prevent the abuse of our children?

The answer is simple. But its implications are complex. Achieving the solution will be difficult and uncomfortable for most of us. What will be asked of us will challenge each of us—just as Moses was challenged, just as the rich young man was challenged.

The difference between those who live abundantly and those who barely live are the choices made along the way.

31

The way of violence is pain and suffering. The way of love is peace and joy. The one brings despair; the other, hope.

Every new parent is asked to make a choice—not between good and bad or right and wrong, but between the ways of violence and the ways of love. By the end of this book, we will be asked to make that choice.

The way we choose will be the legacy we leave our children and grandchildren. Even more important, it will be the life we choose. Life is God's gift to us. What we do with it—how we live it—is our gift to him.

Points to Ponder

1. If I am created in the image of God, do I likewise reflect his qualities?
2. Is there a difference between what I am and the image I reflect?
3. What do I see when I look at myself? What do others see? Does God see something different?
4. Am I afraid of getting too close to people, for fear they will discover the "real me" and be disappointed?
5. Am I so preoccupied with what I do not have that I cannot see or appreciate what I do have?
6. Do I trust God, really?
7. Am I being challenged to surrender my greatest fear in this life in order to fulfill God's purpose for me? If so, what is that fear?
8. Do I have a master in this life, other than Jesus? Is it money, or accomplishments, or fear, or comfort? Is it guilt, or resentment, or desire for revenge?
9. If I were challenged to surrender my earthly master in order to follow Jesus, what would I do?

CHAPTER TWO

Myth 1: *Childhood Is What You Do While You're Waiting to Grow Up!*

It was April 22—just an ordinary day in the lives of most people. But it was no ordinary day for me, or for my daughter. It was her seventh birthday!

This birthday was different from the previous six; several of her friends had come over to share her special day. The party was held in the backyard around a decorated picnic table. I was as excited as any of the children! I had never been to a real birthday party before.

While watching the children laugh their way through several games, resisting the temptation to join them, I began to appreciate just what a wonderful gift God has given us in birthdays. What great opportunities they provide! They allow us to pause for a moment in our frantic pursuits of daily life to celebrate, in a special way, another of God's gifts—children.

And they are a gift! Despite the frustrations and fatigue that often accompany parenthood, it is one of the most profound signs of God's love and trust in us. Imagine! God allows us to take one of his own to raise as one of us. Just as he entrusted the care and nurturing of Jesus to his earthly parents, God calls upon us to raise his other children. What faith he must have in us! What trust! How many of us could trust another to love our children and care for them as we do? But such is God's trust in us!

As I stood there basking in the glow of this thought and watching the children, I became painfully aware of yet another message of birthdays. They serve to remind us that all things change. People change. Tomorrows become todays, and todays become our yesterdays. Children grow up and move on to pursue lives of their own. Life changes. Nowhere is it written that tomorrow will be the same as today. And yet, how often we live as though nothing changes, as though everything will remain forever the same!

I suspect you and I are very much alike in this regard. We become so engrossed in making a living, making ends meet, meeting the endless demands placed upon us, that often we take for granted those things most precious to us. Our feeling seems to be that if we could ever once get caught up, or get ahead just a little, then we could give more attention to our children, our spouses, even our own special needs so long overlooked. In our endless struggle to get ahead, we seem forever to fall behind. The result is that the things we care most about are often those about which we seem to be the most careless!

Absorbed in this thought, I became incredibly aware of how precious this particular moment really was in the life of my daughter. I began to realize that today, with its many joys, must be appreciated for what it is at the moment, instead of squandering it for what tomorrow might bring. Or sacrificing it to the problems of yesterday. Today I have my daughter and can celebrate her life with a party. Tomorrow I may weep for her.

As disturbing as that realization was, it deepened my appreciation of that special moment. No longer taking her for granted, sharing in her birthday became very important.

Crowned with party hats, the children gathered around the table to share in the birthday bonanza of cake, ice cream, and presents. With beaming smiles, they urged Deanna to make a wish and blow out the candles while they sang the happy-birthday song.

Squinting in deep concentration, she finally opened her eyes and, with a mighty rush of wind, blew out all the candles on the cake. The other children cheered, assuring her that whatever she had wished would certainly come true.

Once the children had settled down to the feast, I carelessly asked my daughter the question you should never ask a birthday child:

"If you could have anything in the whole, wide world right now at this moment, what would it be?"

What surprised me most was not that I dared ask the question. You know what they say about fools! What startled me was her answer. She did not hesitate for even a second.

"I wish I was a grown-up!"

To say I was shocked would be an understatement. That was not the response I was expecting! Whatever happened to wishing for riches, or to be the prettiest girl in the country, or for no more school?

After regaining my composure, I just as quickly lost it again by asking another question just as foolish.

"Why in the world would you want to be a grown-up?"

Again there was no hesitation. It was as though this little seven-year-old girl had it all thought out.

"So I could be just like you!"

Be Just Like Me?

If her response to my first question surprised me, the answer to the second propelled me into a whirlwind of troubled thought from which I have yet to escape years later! The thought that my daughter would so gladly surrender her childhood astonished me. That she wanted to be like me was even more astounding!

On the one hand, I was both pleased and flattered that my daughter aspired to be like her dear old papa. Most of us perceive ourselves as models worthy of imitation—at least on our good days! But on the other hand, a part of me cringed in dismay!

Like most parents, what I hope most for my daughter is not that she grow up to be *like* me, but that she become *better* than her father! It did not bother me to think that what strengths I possess could be passed on to her. What is so disturbing is that along with the strengths will go the weaknesses and shortcomings. Caring parents do not desire to leave their children such a legacy.

The truth of the matter is that children do tend to grow up to be amazingly similar to their parents. Whether I like it or not, my daughter is as likely to grow up to be like me as your child is likely to grow up to be like you. She not only will resemble me physically; she is sure to share similar ways of thinking, feeling, expressing herself, perceiving the world around her and other people, believing, and certainly behaving. Much of what I am, she will become! That is unavoidable.

When it comes to human relationships, children learn more from what we do than from what we say. This is a truth many of us tend to forget in our day-to-day parenting.

One of the greatest challenges facing all parents is how

36

best to become strong, healthy role models for our children, knowing full well that we are anything but perfect. Perhaps an equal challenge is how best to help our children derive the most from their childhoods while at the same time preparing for the roles and responsibilities that lie ahead. It is so easy to look past those few special years of childhood to the years of adolescence and adulthood, thereby sacrificing the gifts of today for the promises of tomorrow. Following the example of their parents, children often become so preoccupied with what tomorrow might bring that they overlook the treasures laid out before them today.

A popular marketing device for magazine companies today is the solicitation of new orders through the lure of sweepstakes. The prospective buyer is reminded of the foolish man who literally threw away $1 million. He did not send in his entry because he did not know the possible value of what he held in his hand. In his mind, the chance of winning was so remote, it was no chance at all!

The tragedy is that what appeared to be just another piece of junk mail could have made that man a very wealthy person. Without endorsing such a marketing scheme, we must acknowledge that any chance, however remote, is an opportunity—an opportunity to be either seized or forfeited.

Every waking moment brings us a limitless array of new chances—chances to do or say, to grow, to believe, to learn, to change. Every morning brings us a chance for a new life with a new beginning! A sweepstakes called Life!

The chances come to us in the form of tasks and chores, responsibilities, relationships, jobs, hopes, dreams, ideas. But how many of us recognize these daily events as opportunities, chances to win?

37

Yet, who knows which of the chances we take each day might alter the course of our life? Or the lives of our children? But like the man with the winning sweepstakes number, how are we to know the value of what we hold in our hands? Or in our minds? Or what we see before us or around us? Or even the value of what we hold in our hearts? How can we teach our children to recognize the treasures of childhood when we are blind to the treasures in our own lives?

She Wants to Be an Adult?

My daughter was not unique in wanting to be an adult. In fact, I really should not have been surprised by her response. Most children seem to think they would rather be adults!

How well I remember my own desperate desire to be an adult as I was growing up. If I were an adult, I naively thought then, my parents would not do such awful things; or at least I would be big enough to make some changes in my life that would end the abuse. Like most children, I perceived adulthood as possessing the two most desirable qualities of life: the power to control others and the freedom to control oneself. What children do not yearn for the freedom to do as they please when they please? And what children do not dream of someday having the power to control others as they are controlled?

There a number of reasons children become willing to trade their childhood for adulthood. Let's look at a few of them.

1. *Like Mother, Like Daughter.* Most parents—particularly Americans—tend to look past today for a better tomorrow. Our basic attitude seems to be that whatever tomorrow has to offer is bound to be better than what we

have experienced today. For many, today is the price we must pay for a tomorrow. It is just another day to get through, to survive until that elusive, "better" tomorrow comes along, with its promise of all good things.

This attitude is reflected both in our work and in our play. How many times does the phrase, "I can't wait until—" inadvertently slip into our conversation? How many of us find things to do to help us "pass the time until—"? Sound familiar? Most of us seem willing to forsake much of what today offers in our endless search for tomorrow.

Our children pick up our attitudes. They value what is important to us. How can we expect them to fully appreciate today—their childhood—and live it to the fullest, if they constantly see that we forsake what today offers for what might be tomorrow?

In a real sense, today is all there is. With a hope for tomorrow and the memory of yesterday, today is our life. The way we live each moment will determine our memories and also fashion our hopes and dreams.

No goal is ever achieved until that first step is taken. To overlook the importance of that first ordinary, mundane step, or any step between beginning and end, could very well alter our course through life so that we never would really arrive where we want to go. What a tragedy it is to live in hope of what tomorrow might bring, and then die in despair, realizing what disappeared with yesterday!

2. *Postchildhood Amnesia.* Parents often have unrealistic perceptions of childhood. In their quest to be what others would have them be and to meet the seemingly endless expectations they place upon themselves, many parents literally forget what it was like to be a child. They

suffer from postchildhood amnesia. This peculiar condition tends to manifest itself in two extremes.

On the one hand, some parents glamorize childhood as something out of a fairy tale. They tend to expect too much of children, apparently oblivious to the fact that in addition to being a playground, childhood is equally a battleground for the shaping and developing of young personalities.

These parents tend to be "fair weather" friends to their children, always ready to share the fun, but unable to understand and help when the storm hits, or the going gets tough, or when life throws one of its proverbial curves.

Fairy-tale parents tend to romanticize childhood, seeing only its possibilities, rarely its realities. The result is that they build a protective cocoon around their children to shield them from life, often not recognizing the fine line between sanctuary and prison!

Children in these families usually see and hear and experience only what is allowed by the parent. And they most often see the adults upon whom they must model themselves living peaceful lives full of love and beauty, without problems or trials. To the child struggling alone with inevitable growing pains, adulthood appears to be a perpetual state of untroubled bliss. Is it any wonder the child yearns for that?

At the other extreme are parents who nullify childhood altogether. They perceive it as an inferior condition, a handicap, a deficiency that must be corrected if the child is ever to be happy and successful.

These parents live to become something else, always looking for what might be, rather than accepting what is and making the most of it. They tend to expect too little of their children. Rarely do they see the magic of childhood, but only its difficulties and burdens. What child would not welcome a chance to escape something so dreadful?

It is true that we tend to see what we are looking for in other people, in ourselves, and in our children. Those who look for trouble usuallly find it. And those who look for beauty usually find that!

In both cases it is clear that these parents are not giving their children an accurate view of childhood. Childhood is never all bad or all good. Perhaps parents who glamorize childhood have forgotten some of its hardships. And those who remember only its troubles have forgotten those carefree magical moments that are present in every childhood, whether recognized or not.

Perhaps if we could remember more of our own childhoods, we would allow our children to experience more of theirs. Those of us who grew up in abusive homes might do well to remember, to make sure we do not pass it on to our children. And those who were blessed with happy childhoods also would do well to remember, to make sure we *do* pass it on—to as many children as possible!

3. *What do you want from me?* Some parents rob their children of healthy childhoods by reversing the parent/child roles. The children are called upon to meet their parents' needs for comfort, love, and support. These parents tend to expect too much, asking children to think, feel, or behave beyond their years.

Role reversal can lead to serious consequences. When an adult turns to a child to meet adult needs, the child not only is likely to be exploited, but is also at a much higher risk of being abused. What is likely to happen if the child is unable to meet the demands of the parent? What if the parent believes the child is simply being disobedient? Or stubborn? Or is trying to get even? Or is rejecting the

41

parent? Or what might happen when a parent begins to think of the child as replacing the spouse? This is one of the primary causes of the physical and sexual abuse of children! Adult needs must be met by other adults in adult relationships.

Children who are expected to think and function beyond their developmental capabilities are lured by adult ways of behaving. They receive reward and praise for being or doing as their parents ask. A need to please parents is a primary motivation behind much childhood behavior.

What child would not welcome a chance to be rid of such a distorted childhood? Children seek what appears to be the freedom of adulthood in order to escape the responsibilities and demands of childhood!

4. *Never Good Enough.* Some parents see only deficiency when they look at their children. They see how much the children do not know, what they cannot do, what they are incapable of understanding. They tend to measure parental success by the degree of competence demonstrated by the children, and they spend most of their time with the children trying to correct the deficiencies. Any way in which the children fail implies their own inadequacy—something they cannot and will not tolerate.

As a result, the children feel they are never good enough. No matter what they do or how well they do it, their parents are never satisfied. Most children experience tremendous levels of guilt when they are incapable of being or doing what their parents want. Children want to be a source of pride for their parents, and to escape this guilt, they long for adulthood.

5. *Why don't you grow up?* Some adults experience the dependence of another person as a burden. They understand the basic needs of their children, but may have a

difficult time fulfilling those needs. It is one thing to know, for example, that children cannot control their bowels at an early age, and quite another to assume responsibility for keeping a baby changed and clean.

Many parents do not look at such parts of parenting as necessities of everyday life, but perceive them as burdens that are not only unpleasant, but unfair. They may push a child to be potty-trained at the earliest age possible, regardless of the immediate or long-term consequences.

These parents want their children to grow up too fast, to become independent and self-sufficient as soon as possible. They often equate dependence with personal weakness, and in their minds, the world is a jungle where only the strong survive!

6. *Why don't you control that kid?* Some parents react to the dependency of children by overstructuring their young lives. They attempt to direct all their children's efforts into activities or pursuits they believe worthy of their time and attention. For many adults, controlling the life of another brings a sense of being in control of their own lives.

Childhood may well become a prison in which these children must respond in robotlike fashion to the demands of a heartless taskmaster. They tend to be suffocated by the lack of freedom and spontaneity, and sooner or later will want to escape that oppression.

7. *Parent Martyrs.* Some parents take on the role of the suffering martyr, sacrificing their own needs and wants in order to tend to those of the children—and resenting every minute of it! They constantly remind the children in one way or another just how much personal sacrifice they are making.

As a result, the children usually feel guilty and ashamed

43

and may try to ease the burden of the parent by assuming responsibility for themselves and others before they are capable of doing so.

Children do not want to be a burden to their parents, nor do they want to be the cause of pain and suffering. The knowledge that you bring hurt to those you love, simply because you exist, would motivate almost any child to want to forfeit childhood.

8. *It's only child's play.* It would be easy for most of us to consider childhood activities unimportant. While it is true that some are more important than others, some parents tend to see all such activities and events as basically unimportant; only their own concerns rate special attention.

As noted earlier, children tend to value those things that are important to the parents. If childhood activities do not gain the parents' special attention, their children will not consider them important enough to deserve special effort. These children often try to substitute adult pursuits because they are the only ones that receive parental attention and praise.

Many parents misunderstand the nature of play. Play is the occupation of childhood. It is pursued with a level of intensity and commitment similar to an adult's pursuit of a career. From play, children learn many lessons about life, relationships, and the nature of reality. Play is as vital to the development of a healthy personality as are food and exercise for the development of a healthy body.

Some of us may try to discourage play or replace it with something else, or we may merely tolerate it as the foolishness of childhood. This could be a serious mistake. Play, exploration, and fantasy, within safe limits, are very important parts of any healthy childhood and should not be discouraged. Out of these grow the hope and inspiration of adulthood.

Little Adults

It is a common mistake to see future adults when we look at our children. This is unavoidable, to some extent, in that all conscientious parents think and plan for their children's future. The danger is that, in looking past childhood to the future, we may miss childhood altogether—or we could very well destroy it!

We could seriously harm our children and distort their childhood in several ways:

1. We may be so concerned about the social, educational, romantic, and vocational aspects of their future that we regard childhood merely as a training ground. In this case, we run the risk of manipulating the experiences of our children as though they are pawns in a chess match, in which sacrifice of the moment is necessary to achieve ultimate success.

2. We may project upon our children our own unfulfilled hopes, dreams, and aspirations in an attempt to reclaim or relive our own lives through them, pushing them to be and do what we could not.

3. We may project our own weaknesses, faults, and inadequacies upon our children. How easy it is for us to see laziness or a tendency toward dishonesty, if that happens to be our failing. This dynamic is particularly dangerous, in that most parents feel perfectly justified, if not compelled, to punish their children in an effort to correct deficiencies and build character. The punishment too often becomes harsh and damaging, resulting in child abuse.

4. We may push our children to grow up too soon. We

live in a world where, more and more, children are being faced with serious adult concerns and stresses. We expect them to deal with these vital issues with the maturity, wisdom, and self-control of seasoned adults. What is more, they do deal with them—and in much the same way as their adult models—through alcohol and drug abuse, running away, suicide, promiscuity, mental illness, acting out, and a host of other self-destructive behaviors.

We need only listen to the adult themes being expressed endlessly in our children's music and cartoons, being flaunted in the television commercials which advertise their shirts, shoes, and jeans. There we find a sense of the incredible adult temptations they face.

It is not enough to protect our children. We must protect their childhood as well. The role of the environment in shaping human personality is well known. Adult personalities are largely shaped by childhood experiences. They become the foundation upon which we build the rest of our lives.

Children need to be loved and appreciated as much for what they are today as for what they may become tomorrow. One of the greatest gifts a parent can give is a secure, happy childhood—the freedom to be a child.

Childhood is not what we do while we are waiting to grow up. Growing up is what we do while we are living our childhood to its fullest!

Points to Ponder

1. Is the experience of raising children a sign of God's faith and trust in me? Is it more often an opportunity for me? Or a burden?

2. Do I tend to be careless about the very things most important to me? My children? My spouse?

3. Do I really want my children to grow up to be just like me? How would I want them to be different? The same?

4. Which teaches my children the stronger lesson: What I say? Or how I live?

5. Do I suffer from postchildhood amnesia? Have I forgotten what it's like to be a child? Would I be more sensitive to my children and their needs if I did remember?

6. What motivates my children to behave as they do? A desire to please me? To please themselves? Because it is the "right" thing to do?

7. Do I allow my children to be children—to play and be carefree? Or do I push them to grow up too soon?

8. How much of what I do and say today will affect the kind of adults my children will become? Do I say and do things that hurt instead of help?

9. What do I see when I look into the face of my child? An incomplete adult? Or a child?

CHAPTER THREE

Myth 2: *Parenting Is the Most Natural Thing in the World! Anybody Can Do It!*

It was Easter eve, 1973. Since it was a holiday weekend, I had been called in to work early and asked to stay till closing. It was going to be a long shift. Travelers along the main highway had kept our fast-food restaurant busy all day.

I was twenty-three and a full-time student at the college on the outskirts of town. That meant I had to work nights to support myself and my wife. I was lucky to find a job with the restaurant so near the school. With many students needing work, competition was tough.

I worked hard, and in less than a year I was promoted to assistant manager in charge of the night shift. Despite the promotion, my three dollars per hour was barely enough, but I was determined to stay in school and grateful for the job.

By the time we closed at midnight that Saturday, I had already worked a twelve-hour shift, and then we had to clean up. It was close to two o'clock in the morning by the time I finally climbed into my car and drove the dozen miles along the winding road to the house Wendy and I rented in the country.

At first I was surprised to see all the lights on in the house. But surprise quickly evaporated into fatigue as I remembered the many nights Wendy would get up alone to relieve the discomfort of her heavy burden. She was pregnant with our first child and due any day.

Turning off the ignition, I sat in the silent darkness a moment before getting out. Somehow I had a feeling that my day was not over. The baby was going to come tonight!

An icy chill raced up my spine and settled as a frozen knot of horror in my brain at the thought of becoming a father. It terrified me. My fear was not for myself, but for the child. My greatest fear was that I would be like my own adopted father, do to my child what had been done to me. I would rather be dead than become like him!

Regaining my composure, I entered the house. Wendy, carrying the bag she had packed weeks before, met me and, with few words, ushered me back to the car. The contractions were only short minutes apart, and she was urgent in her plea that I get her to the hospital as quickly as possible.

I paced away the hours of labor in the waiting room, along with another nervous father-to-be, chain-smoking my way into a fierce headache. Occasionally fatigue would overtake me and I would collapse nervously into the chair beside the window that overlooked the hospital grounds.

My mind was a jumble of confused, tangled thoughts as I was at last forced to deal with impending fatherhood. Throughout the months of pregnancy I had been able to avoid the issue by staying occupied with the demands of school and work. But the time had come when it could be avoided no longer. Within hours—perhaps minutes—I

49

would have a child to raise. Not a dog or a cat or some other lovable pet, but a child—a human being who had to be fed and clothed and sheltered and taught all the things necessary for survival in this world. And I was the one who had to do it all! But how? I didn't know the first thing about being a parent.

Along with everything else, my obvious incompetence frightened me. What if I did something wrong that would hurt the child? Or what if I did not know the right thing to do in case of an emergency? What if I just did not have what it takes to be a parent?

Mingled with feelings of inadequacy and fear was a deep personal shame for having procreated a child without first being prepared for parenthood. Why hadn't I taken the time to attend those parenting classes offered through the hospital? I had kept telling myself I would get to it later. Later never came. But the baby had! Prepared or not, I soon would be a parent.

Along with the fear, the thought of becoming a father intrigued me. I was overcome by a growing sense of my own personal importance. All my life I had sought desperately to be wanted and needed and loved. Maybe now, just maybe, I would be needed! Maybe the child would love me as no on else could. Perhaps the child would give me that sense of worthiness I so desperately needed. Growing out of a childhood of violence and abuse in which I was made to feel unloved and unwanted, it was a dim hope, but a fascinating one, and it reawakened within me a host of infantile hopes and dreams.

But at the same time, I felt a growing sense of dread and foreboding. Unlike the fear I had known as a child, this fear was for someone else. Someone not yet born. Someone even more dependent and helpless than I had been. Barely able to care for myself and Wendy, how was I to meet the incredible needs of a totally dependent child? What kind of father would I be, when the only father I had known had very nearly destroyed me?

But underlying the fear, like a swift, dangerous current, was a terror that only the betrayed innocence of a child can know, a terror that arose from my own childhood of helplessness and abuse.

Feeling as though I were drowning in a sea of swirling emotions, I fought against both a tension that seemed to strangle me and the incredible desire to bolt from that place and never return. It took all the courage I could muster to sit there, awaiting the moment I would be introduced to a person whose needs far exceeded my own and whose life would depend on me.

Buried deep in these and a million similar thoughts, I was only vaguely aware of the crimson light that streaked the sky as Easter morning dawned, and it took several seconds for a voice to penetrate the faraway, icy depths of my mind. The words came to me slowly at first, like a distant echo.

"Phil?" At last I heard the female voice clearly.

I jerked around from the window, tipped over the chair as I tried to stand up, and watched in frozen horror as a nurse approached with a small, snugly wrapped bundle.

"Yes, yes! That's me!" I gasped in a raspy voice barely above a whisper.

Smiling warmly, the nurse came close and carefully pulled the blanket away from the face of a baby.

"Phil, I would like you to met your daughter!" she said.

A daughter! It was a girl! I could hardly stand still as a mighty rush of joy swelled from deep inside.

I knew that lying before me was a miracle more wondrous than the mind could possibly imagine.

I thought I was going to faint as the nurse carefully placed the bundle of mystery and magic into my awkward hands. Cradling her carefully in the crook of my arm, holding her close, I was so overwhelmed with emotion I could not speak for several moments as I stared into the sleeping face of the most beautiful baby girl in all the world! She was the most perfect thing I had ever seen! My heart swelled with joy and love, and awe at the miracle of her.

And yet, underlying it all was another feeling; a feeling I dared not admit even to myself until recently; a feeling that made me finally push the baby back into the arms of the waiting nurse. It was a feeling that filled me with dread and personal loathing. It was a feeling of power. Incredible power. Life-and-death power. Total and absolute power over another human being.

As we stood there lost alone together in a world created just for the two of us, I suddenly knew that I had total and absolute control of that child's life. She was my possession. I could do with her as I pleased, and no one would dare challenge my right or my reason for doing so. It was as though I were a god—powerful and omnipotent—in whose hands lay her life and her destiny.

But what sickened me and sent me racing out of the waiting room into the dark courtyard was a vision. As I stood there holding the child I already loved more than anything in the world, her tiny, beautiful head cupped protectively in the palm of my hand, into my mind came a vision of that hand slowly closing around her head until I crushed it.

Outside in the dark, I vomited, then cried myself into total exhaustion.

The Dark Side of Parenting

As with most people who grow up with abuse and exploitation, I possessed a dark side that rarely showed itself in adult relationships. Where there existed a balance of power, few expectations, and a minimum of intimacy, I seemed able to function adequately, without serious threat to myself or anyone else.

But something dramatic occurs when the total and absolute helplessness of a child comes into relationship with the total and absolute power of a parent. The healthy adult will respond in an empathic manner, providing the care, nurture, and protection essential for the child's survival. This is the desired response.

But in an unhealthy person like myself, the response might be quite different. Even as a young adult I remained a tortured and abused child, locked within memories. Those experiences largely determined the way I related to other people—especially those who reminded me of my own helplessness and vulnerability as a child. Instead of triggering a healthy, empathic response, the memories of those experiences could result in an abusive and exploitive response.

Which of the two responses will occur when a child is born into a family depends largely upon the quality of our childhood experiences and the level of empathy we possess. Being able to experience vicariously another's pain or suffering or need or hope or joy is the single most important quality present in any healthy relationship. This is particularly true when it comes to parenting.

Empathy is the feeling that stimulates love and inhibits hate; inspires touching but limits violence; seeks the good in all things, while controlling the bad. It is the emotional strength that binds any relationship and the salve for its perpetual healing. Empathy is the seed for hope, the fuel for change, and the foundation for peace. For out of empathy flows compassion!

The Vital Role of Empathy

The vital role empathy plays in healthy human relationships can be dramatized by observing it in action. What is it that motivates a parent to pick up a child who has stumbled and fallen? Or motivates a community to rally around a bereaved family? Or to celebrate a team victory? What is it that makes us cry when others cry, laugh when they laugh, hurt when they hurt? It is empathy—our ability to share the feelings of another person.

While we lived in an apartment complex several years ago, my daughter developed a strong friendship with another girl, the only child of a single mother. As time went on, the girl's mother spent more and more time away from home. On many of those occasions she would leave her daughter in our care. I spent more than one night holding and rocking that ten-year-old girl while she cried herself to sleep. How desperately she needed her mother! I wonder if I would have been able to respond so compassionately to that child's need if I had not been left alone with strangers myself as a child? I knew from my own childhood experience what she was experiencing. I shared her hurt.

In addition to making it possible for us to share with others at intimate emotional levels, empathy serves to inhibit violence and aggression. As the empathetic person receives pain signals from another—physical or emotional symptoms such as bleeding, tears, sweat, fear or pain in the eyes—it triggers memories of similar feelings in our own lives. We begin to experience vicariously some of the pain and suffering of the other person; it is our own suffering, caused by watching another suffer, that prompts us to ease up, to calm down, to back off.

Empathy makes us so uncomfortable with someone else's suffering that we are motivated to do something about it. Parents unable to empathize with the hurts of their children are likely to do little to relieve the suffering. The result for the child could well be traumatic.

All parents say and do things to their children in times of great anger, frustration, fatigue, or crisis that they would never say or do to another adult. During such times, it is often our ability to empathize that keeps us from going "too far" and causing the child serious harm. High levels of empathy are a must for all parents!

Empathy is learned most easily in childhood. The tragedy for me, as for many others, is that I was never provided the opportunity to develop empathy. My child-hood was spent trying to survive—not only the abuse, but my own incredible feelings. I was too preoccupied with my own feelings to be concerned about those of others. It took all my concentration and effort to avoid being over-whelmed by a childhood that threatened almost daily to destroy me.

Even at the age of twenty-three it was difficult to vicariously experience what someone else might be thinking or feeling. Like other survivors of child abuse, I tended to measure the suffering of others—particularly my children—by my own experience. If what they seemed

55

to be experiencing fell within the range of my own negative experience, then no empathic response would result.

Like all children learning to walk and run and play, my children would occasionally fall down and skin their elbows and knees. Also like most children, they would turn to me for comfort. At first. But after a while they stopped coming to me for comfort. Why? I was totally oblivious to their suffering! Seeing their little skinned elbows and knees provoked no emotional reaction in me at all.

I was relating to the hurts of my children out of my own experience. Compared to the pain I had suffered, what was a skinned elbow or knee? It was nothing—little more than a minor inconvenience!

To be an effective parent, I literally had to resensitize myself to the experiences of my children; to realize that skinned elbows and knees *do* hurt and that it was important to respond with empathy and caring. It took time and conscious effort to develop these empathic skills, but I made it!

What is most frightening is the fact that most victims of severe violence tend to measure the amount of pain and suffering they inflict upon their children by their own experience. If what they are doing to a child, for example, falls within their own experience of childhood, then it is not abusive. If it was good enough for my parents and me, they reason, then it is good enough for me and my child. It is one way to parent, or at least it is the way it has always been done in my family.

This is one reason abused children tend to become abusive parents. We learn how to be parents by watching our own parents. Abusive parenting can be taught as surely as positive parenting can be taught. We teach our children what we learn as children.

The dark side of me that showed itself the night my daughter was born was fueled by the rage of an adult survivor of years of severe child abuse. It enveloped my relationship with her because of the abusive parenting model that had been provided me. It was made evil by its desire for revenge. But the dark side is so dangerous because of its incredible lack of empathy. Evil knows no compassion.

Can Anyone Be an Effective Parent?

Contrary to popular opinion, parenting—beyond the provision of the basic necessities of life—is *not* the most natural thing in the world. The drive to procreate is instinctive and natural. But the knowledge and skills needed to raise children to become successful adults must be learned.

As children, we must learn to walk, to talk, to feed ourselves, to control our behavior as well as our bodily functions. And we must learn to relate to other people. In short, we must learn the essentials of survival and the skills of successful living.

If we, as children, must learn these things for ourselves, how is it possible for us, as adults, to teach them without some help or preparation? Teaching is a profession for which many people spend years preparing themselves. It involves more than just words and actions; it involves mind, heart, body, and soul in the development of knowledge, skills, faith, and understanding.

Tragically, parenthood seems to be the only universal occupation that does not require some kind of training. We must be licensed to drive a car, to practice a profession, even to marry. But nothing is required of us to become

57

parents. And yet, nothing we could possibly do is more important than the way we raise our children.

The prevailing myth in our society is that if a person is capable of procreating a child, then that person is fully capable of raising the child to healthy adulthood. The truth of the matter is that the skills required to procreate are quite different from those required to parent!

As difficult as it may be for some of us to accept, not every person is capable of being an effective parent. Some individuals should never have children.

It is easy to see the potential risk to a child whose parents are mentally ill or insanely violent, severely retarded, trapped in alcoholism or narcotics abuse, or have a history of abuse or exploitation of children. And there are those who have children but do not want them; those who have children but are ill-equipped financially or emotionally to raise them.

It is just as possible for careless parents to twist a child's thinking as it is to twist an arm. It is just as possible to bruise and distort emotions as to damage a hand or foot. It is also possible to damage children spiritually so severely that they become spiritual cripples. Parental ignorance and carelessness is one of the leading causes of permanent damage to children.

The way we raise our children could very well have a direct effect on the quality of life in our community, state, nation, even in the world. It is just as possible to raise a child who strives for peace as one who yearns for war; a child who sees good and beauty in all things as one who knows only the bad and ugly; a child who works to build as one who seeks to destroy. It is just as possible to raise a child who will become President of the United States as to raise one who will kill a President.

If children are our future, then that future is being shaped at this very moment in thousands of homes across the world. In how many of those homes are children going hungry? Or witnessing violence between their parents? Or being physically, emotionally, and sexually abused?

Most child abuse, however, is not the result of malevolence, maliciousness, or a desire to hurt, cripple, or destroy a child. Most abusive parents love their children and desperately want to be good parents. The truth is that most child abuse is rooted in ignorance and tradition—ignorance because the parent knows no other way to parent; tradition because that is the way it always has been done in that family.

But ignorance can be overcome with education; traditions can change. Childhood can be made safe and wholesome by parents who have learned not only to care, but to care effectively.

All parents make mistakes that in one way or another may hurt their children. In most cases those hurts can heal. What should concern us are those mistakes that result in damage to the child: mistakes made through ignorance or carelessness; mistakes that cripple or destroy; mistakes that should never happen.

Child abuse does more than cause hurts. It damages. It leaves scars that never go away, damage that never heals. It is permanent. Severe and prolonged child abuse usually results in perpetual physical, mental, spiritual, or emotional limps in an already troubled and desperate life.

Because of my history of violence and abuse, the emotional problems that plagued me as a result, my poor parenting knowledge and skills, the abusive parenting model provided me, and the economic and social deprivation of my life at twenty-three, I was a poor candidate for fatherhood at the time my daughter was born. It was truly a miracle that I was able to break the cycle of abuse before it resulted in permanent tragedy for all of us.

Is It Our Inalienable Right to Have Children?

To suggest that not all persons should be free to have children is sure to stir a hotly contested debate. We live in an age when individual rights seem to be most important. Battle cries that demand and defend our "rights" are heard with deafening effect in courtrooms and legislative halls across the country. Some will say that the right to have children, regardless of condition or circumstance, is an inalienable human right, guaranteed by our birth into the human race.

From a secular perspective, this may be true. The right to procreate is inherent in the ability to copulate. But those of us who have children know there is a great deal more involved in parenting children than in conceiving them! The right to express one's sexuality carries with it the moral injunction to do so wisely and responsibly, with equal regard for the partner and the potential child.

The situation appears to be quite different when considered from a spiritual perspective. It is not an inalienable human right to have children. Who among us would dare to stand before God and demand human rights? The truth is that we have no "rights" before God—not as individuals, nor as a class of people, nor as a nation, nor as anything. What we have before God is nothing more or less than what he has given us and what we have made of it.

It is our inalienable right to *try* to have children. But nowhere is it written that God must comply with our wishes. If we are blessed with a child, we have received a gift from God—not as our just due, but a precious gift, to be loved, nurtured, and treasured for a time.

What is most certain but perhaps least acknowledged—and certainly not demanded as an inalienable human right—is the responsibility that comes with children. It is the responsibility of parents to provide for, protect, and take care of children until they are capable of taking care of themselves, to teach them the things necessary for life and salvation.

Rarely in our unending quest for self, for personal rights and privileges, do we seek or even acknowledge the duties and responsibilities that are the necessary prerequisites of any right. To exercise a right without responsibility is abuse. When parents are given absolute authority over children and the right to raise them as they choose, without also assigning the explicit responsibility to protect, preserve, and prepare those children for successful adulthood, the parents are set up for failure, and the child for abuse.

Becoming a Parent

Parents must be concerned with all aspects of a child's growth and development—moral and spiritual, as well as physical, mental, and emotional.

Several basic forces shape the kind of parents we become:

1. *Parenting Imprints.* Parenting imprints are those cultural values, beliefs, and practices that help to influence the way we raise our children. Not every human culture, for example, uses spanking as a way to control children. In this country many people do, because of our heritage, our traditions, and even some of our lines of religious teaching. Parents practice a particular parenting

technique because society accepts, condones, perhaps even encourages its use.

Ironically, it is our cultural society that defines what it means to be a "good" parent. It also sets the limits of acceptable and unacceptable practice. Society condones spanking but has made physical abuse a crime. The tragedy for many American families is that they do not know the difference. When they practice what they believe society preaches, the police often must step in to keep the family from destroying itself!

2. *Parenting Program.* A parenting program is like a computer program. The database—the storehouse of knowledge upon which we base our parenting—is an attitude embedded in us by our own parents as we grow up.

Angry parents, for example, tend to treat their children the same way their own angry parents treated them. They tend to punish for the same reasons and use the same kinds of punishment.

While growing up, we learn what it means to be a child, a mother, a father. We learn what is important in families and what is not, how best to keep the family functioning, and how to deal with one another in times of crisis, distress, anger, and conflict.

3. *The Master's Touch.* Master parent is the highest level a mother or father can achieve. Master parents go beyond the minimum requirements of care and nurture for their children. Their concern is not only that their children survive, but that they thrive!

It is at this level that we, as individual human beings, bring to the parenting task that spark of creativity and magic that is uniquely our own. Master parents find time to spend with their children. They seek positive ways of relating, rather than negative, harsh, punishing forms of interaction. They make it possible for their children to explore and experience the world around them, to learn and grow and become all it is possible for them to be. A master parent is a carpenter, an engineer, a teacher, a psychologist, and certainly a sculptor, who slowly etches, carves, and shapes a developing personality, instilling the values and belief structure that will become a firm foundation upon which children can build the rest of their lives.

The ability to parent effectively is not instinctive, but learned. As in all learning, it is just as possible to learn positive ways of doing things as to learn negative ways; just as possible to learn nurturing techniques as abusive. Which will be learned is determined primarily by which is taught.

One of the more tragic legacies of child abuse and domestic violence is that children learn it is all right to hit family members as long as it is done for their own good and because they love them.

It is a serious mistake to believe that parenting is the most natural thing in the world. Such a notion breeds perpetual ignorance and a reluctance to change. It is our ignorance and the blind clinging to unchanging tradition that could spell doom for modern parents and tragedy for our children.

Points to Ponder

1. Am I an empathetic parent? What areas in my children's lives are easiest for me to relate to at a personal level? What are some areas that I find it very difficult to relate to?

2. Do I sometimes say and do things to my children that I would not dream of doing or saying to another adult? What are they?

3. Did I learn to be a parent by watching my parents? How am I similar to them? How am I different?

4. How much time and energy am I willing to put in to become a better parent? In what areas of parenting would I benefit most from parenting education?

5. Do I believe that having children is an inalienable right? Do I own my children? Am I entirely free to do with them as I choose?

6. What are the responsibilities that accompany the opportunity to have children? Which do I assume well? Which responsibilities am I reluctant to assume?

7. How do I decide when and how to punish my children? How do I know when enough is enough?

8. How does my culture influence how I raise my children? Which of its values and beliefs do I want to pass on to my children? Which do I not want to pass on?

9. Can anyone parent successfully? What makes some parents more effective than others?

CHAPTER FOUR

Myth 3: *What That Kid Needs Is a Good Spanking!*

Little is known about Barabbas, the man who stood with Jesus to be judged by the crowd that Passover day so long ago. There is reason to believe he was a member of the radical Jewish Zealots who were attempting to overthrow Roman rule and that he had been arrested for insurrection and murder. In any case, he clearly represents the darkest forces of the human spirit—violence and danger.

Imagine the scene. Jerusalem was overflowing with people who had come to celebrate the Feast of the Passover. The mood was festive as families and friends were reunited within the protective walls of the holy city. But the mood was also serious, for this was a celebration of the time God had called Moses from his wilderness exile to lead the enslaved Hebrew people out of Egyptian bondage. When the angel of death was sent into Egypt to claim the lives of all the firstborn children, God had shown mercy to his faithful and obedient people by instructing the angel to pass over their homes.

Sensitive to the political unrest Jesus had caused among the chief priests and scribes, Pilate decided to use the milling Passover crowds to satisfy the demands of the Jewish authorities that Jesus be arrested and also to administer Roman justice. So as not to offend Rome or the Temple, Pilate chose to let the people decide the fate of Jesus.

After seating himself on his throne of judgment high above the anxious crowds, Pilate called for Barabbas to be brought out and placed on his left. Then Jesus was brought forth to stand on his right. After the crowd had been silenced, Pilate asked the people which of the two men he should release.

More than a choice between two accused men, it was a choice between good and evil, the ways of Barabbas and the ways of Jesus. On Pilate's left stood the human embodiment of deceit, violence, and murder; on his right, the human incarnation of truth, peace, and love. Both men were condemned by the state. Both were well known to the people. Some scholars believe both men were named Jesus. Yet one would be shown mercy and the other would die.

The choice was the same for the people then as it is for us today. Whom do we choose, the Jesus called Barabbas or the Jesus called Christ?

It is likely that Barabbas embodied more of the characteristics the people of his day found desirable. He had a commanding presence and was conspiring to overthrow their Roman rulers. He represented power to an oppressed, helpless people.

Jesus, on the other hand, challenged the people's traditions and ways of thinking. He forced them to look at themselves. He taught a new way of life—a way of peace and love. And he, too, offered power to an oppressed, helpless people: He taught that the meek would inherit the earth.

What the people of that day failed to recognize is the same thing we fail to see today. The power offered by following in the footsteps of Barabbas is an illusion that will destroy us. The way of Barabbas is filled with violence and suffering. To follow him is to walk the path to death. To choose Jesus is to choose the way of love and peace. To walk in his path is to walk the way of life, the way of Truth. His way is the only way, if we are to survive.

While celebrating their own merciful deliverance from Egyptian tyranny, violence, and death, the people made their choice. They chose Barabbas.

The Choices We Make

There is nothing we can do to change history. As much as most of us would like to try occasionally, we cannot go back and undo what has been done. The past is an unchanging reality with which we must live. We cannot change the choice of the people that cost our Lord his life, and we cannot change the choices of some parents that cost children their childhood. The only control we have is over our own choices. We can choose to uplift and preserve life as a holy and sacred gift—or we can choose to degrade and destroy it.

Jesus died violently. When Pilate asked what should be done with him, they yelled, "Crucify him!"

Crucifixion—nailed or bound to a cross to die, sometimes head down—was one of the most brutal punishments, and it always was preceded by scourging. In choosing to spare Barabbas, the people not only chose to preserve evil and destroy good, but they sanctioned violence as an acceptable method of resolving human problems.

They, like Barabbas, became guilty of murder.

Would our Lord have died that awful death if the people around him had not condoned the use of crucifixion as acceptable punishment for convicted criminals? Would he have been scourged and beaten if the people had not sanctioned the use of violence? Would he have known less agony if the people had been more compassionate? Even more frightening, could the words, "Crucify him!" spring as quickly to our lips today?

Not a day passes that each of us does not make similar choices. We must choose between good and evil, right and wrong; we must decide how best to accomplish our goals and meet our needs. This is particularly true in our relationships with people—especially those in our families. Always, there are problems. Always, there are difficulties, misunderstandings, conflicts. Always, we must find effective ways to resolve those problems. And all too often, the way we choose includes the use of violence.

How many times have we stood in the crowd, shouting with the others, "Execute him!"? How many times have we stood in the mob and heard ourselves scream, "Hit him again!"? How many times have we told our children that the best way to deal with someone who has hit them is to hit back? Haven't we learned yet that violence perpetuates violence? That the way to stop violence is not to use it? How many times have we hit our children because we love them?

Jesus said, "Truly, I say to you, as you did it to one of the least of these my brethren, you did it to me" (Matt. 25:40). If we believe this to be true, we must know that every act of violence directed at another, regardless of age, is an act of violence directed at Jesus.

Every time we lift our hand or voice against a child or an adult, the result is a suffering that transcends all time and space—a suffering as real for Jesus today as it was during that Passover holiday so long ago. Just as love is a universal emotion that binds all peoples to our Lord, so too is pain.

Violence in Family Life

Violence was not uncommon in the days of Jesus. Whether forced upon the people by war or civil unrest or sought out as a form of recreation or entertainment in the coliseum, violence was a part of everyday life.

Little has changed. Violence still influences the way we live. Many believe violence is an acceptable form of punishment and an effective way to solve problems between people.

As a result, there is no place in all of society more dangerous than the American home. Rather than a haven of peace and security, for many people their home is a prison of suffering and despair. People are more likely to be attacked, beaten, sexually or emotionally abused, or even killed by another family member than by someone outside the home. This is a shocking truth that many of us continue to deny while others struggle to survive.

Like Barabbas and his followers, we seem to believe that we can achieve power and justice by violence; that the ways of force are more effective than the ways of love. We kill in the name of justice, fight for the sake of honor, and amass huge armies with staggering destructive potential to control the world. We will even pay a man several million dollars to climb into a padded ring and beat another human being into senselessness. The purpose? To demonstrate to an admiring audience the strength and power of one man over another.

Our national preoccupation with violence does not stop

69

in the ring. Violence is in our music, our art, our movies, our literature. Sadly, it is also in our hearts and minds and spills over into the way we treat one another. We tolerate it, accept it, sanction it, practice it, and, in some instances, encourage and demand it. As a good and noble people, we have been persuaded to praise and worship the very evil force that is destroying us!

Some of us live each day in a desperate attempt to survive the violence that is so much a part of our lives. Is it really so hard to understand why so many of us die? Why so many families are destroyed? Can we not see the effects of violence in the crippled minds, bodies, and spirits of those all around us who survive in silent desperation?

Why Do We Choose Violence?

It is hard to understand why we inflict upon our loved ones the very abuses we pay a massive police force to protect us from outside the home. We excuse acts and words from family members that never would be tolerated from a stranger.

The tragedy for many families is that by overlooking abuses, they perpetuate them. Abuse, once begun, is sure to continue and become more severe. Mild violence used to control children, for example, can escalate over the years into severe violence used in an attempt to control an adolescent or adult. What may have started as parents' effort to preserve the family can eventually destroy it.

Families feel justified in using violence to control their members for several reasons, although most of these rationalizations are rooted in ignorance and tradition.

1. *Violence is socially accepted.* Our country was born in the midst of violent revolution and grew to its present size

through expansion that conquered all in its way. Several costly wars have been fought to protect ourselves and others, and uprisings, demonstrations, and violent protests are not uncommon.

Just as we maintain a modern military force unmatched in history to protect us from enemies outside our borders, so too must we maintain a massive police force within our nation to protect us from ourselves and one another! The cost is incredible.

Despite the everyday violence in our society that results in suffering, loss of life, and a tremendous financial burden for taxpayers, most adult Americans believe it is acceptable to use some violence in raising children. Many believe that parenting is an impossible task without it, or that when a parent is too permissive there is a risk of spoiling the child.

Not long ago I had the misfortune of being in a supermarket when a young mother was confronted with what all parents must deal with sooner or later. When she refused her small son a cookie, the child burst into tears and sat down in the middle of the aisle. In an effort to move the boy out of the way of other shoppers, the mother tried to lift him to his feet, but the child stiffened his legs and refused to budge. His crying became more frantic.

The woman, becoming frustrated herself, glanced quickly at the faces around her. She must have sensed the silent expectation, a message that she get the child under control, and soon.

I watched with pity as she desperately threatened and pleaded. Soon her words became harsh, and the louder she yelled, the louder the child cried.

Feeling the unseen pressure to be the good parent those

71

around her expected her to be, the mother was near panic herself. Unable to get the child to stop crying or even get up off the floor, she at last jerked him up by one arm and landed two solid swats on his small bottom.

I sensed a collective sigh of relief from the other shoppers and a noticeable easing of tension. It was as though they could all relax, now that the mother had done the "right" thing. At last she had done what they would have done!

Although the child was standing now and begging to be picked up, the mother refused, for fear of appearing to "give in." The blows had done nothing to stop the crying, but only made it more desperate. And at last the woman bolted from the store, dragging the screaming child by one arm.

What could have been a pleasant outing for mother and child had turned into a disaster, an experience neither would soon forget. It had damaged their relationship rather than enhancing it.

As the woman left the store, I heard one shopper say to another, loudly enough for all to hear, "What that kid needs is a good spanking!"

No one disagreed. It was as though the final word had been spoken and there was nothing more to discuss. The solution to the problem, they seemed to be saying, was to spank the child until he stopped crying.

I wondered if the mother would have handled the situation any differently had she not been in public under the watchful and critical eye of peers. Without the pressure of social expectations, would she have felt free to *discipline* her son rather than *punish* him? Could she have turned a potentially harmful situation into a moment to be remembered, instead of one they would never forget?

What do you suppose would have happened if, when the child had first asked for the cookie, the mother had said, "No, it's too close to supper time. But you can have this [hand child a food item] to put in the basket for me"? Or if she had said, "You can have either a small box of raisins or a package of nuts. Which do you want?" Or if she had hugged the child and said, "I know you would like a cookie. I would like one too. But we'll both just have to wait until we get home to get something to eat."

Power struggles between children and parents should be avoided if possible. Rarely does a clear winner emerge. But if there is a winner, there also will be loser, and winning at the expense of others is not a healthy lesson to teach children—nor is hitting as a way to control others.

2. *Violence is glamorized.* Only a medium that deals entirely with fantasy and illusion can make violence directed at another human being seem pretty, sexy, funny, glamorous, an opportunity for romance and adventure, or an expression of love. And yet that is precisely what occurs on the television screen in most American homes every night.

Average American children will spend almost twice as much time watching television as they do in school. Is it any wonder they seek to model themselves after the heroes on the screen? Is it any wonder they try to dress and act like the characters they admire? Or that they model their values and beliefs on them? Is it really such a mystery why several young people kill themselves playing Russian roulette after watching their movie hero do the same thing and walk away?

Repeated romanticizing of violence on the screen decreases our horror of it. We experience the painless illusion and are invited to feel only the thrill of its incredible power. Who among us would not like to walk fearlessly among the masses, a Samson of strength and courage, commanding respect and adoration?

Seeing the strength of imaginary idols or observing the extraordinary sensuality of a television temptress heightens our own feelings of inadequacy. Is it any wonder we would want to be like them, have what they possess? The more desirable the honey, the less frightening the bee!

3. *Violence is taught.* Some child-care specialists and educators actually teach the use of controlled violence as a solution to parent/child conflicts, as a way to build character or as an effective teaching method. Rarely do these professionals question the ethics or the long-term effectiveness of the practice. There is an underlying assumption that since it has been the custom for so many years, then not only must it be acceptable, but it also must work!

But it is faulty reasoning to assume that a way of doing something is right simply because it always has been done that way. Studies have shown that spanking children is, in the long run, one of the least effective of all parenting techniques and undoubtedly one of the most dangerous!

4. *Violence is modeled in relationships.* Our modern schools teach us how to make a living, but they do not teach us how to live. Yet some of our most serious problems involve finding ways to live together in peace. This applies to relationships both outside and within the home.

Almost 50 percent of American marriages will end in divorce. Marriages are relationships established willingly, and if we do not have the knowledge and skills—and commitment—needed to make these voluntary relationships successful, how can we expect to be successful at those that are not a matter of our own choosing?

Negotiating relationships, dealing with anger, and resolving interpersonal conflicts involve social skills learned in the family. Most of us grew up in families where at least some violence was used as an acceptable force in getting along with other people.

Many of us watched our parents hit each other or suffered through the violence used against us, all the while being told it was done out of love. We grew up believing that hitting is an acceptable way to express anger, get what we want, or control others.

I will never forget the first time I hit my oldest daughter. She was barely a year old. My brother, on leave from the Marine Corps, was staying at the home of my adoptive parents, and Wendy and I had accepted an invitation to visit.

At first my infant daughter crawled curiously around the room, her dancing eyes searching out faces and places. At last they came to rest on the decorative objects on the coffee table in front of us. She crawled to the table and struggled to pull herself to her feet. Standing at last on wobbly legs, the child was just tall enough to reach those objects.

Wanting to show my parents I was a responsible parent, I cautioned the child several times about touching the objects on the table. She would look at me with beautiful brown, innocent eyes and flash me a gorgeous smile. But as soon as the conversation in the room picked up again, she would continue her exploration.

I could feel the tension of disapproval growing in my parents. They expected me to make the child stop touching

75

the objects. But how? It was obvious that merely telling her to stop did not work. The child was not old enough to know what I was saying.

I became more and more uncomfortable as the seconds ticked off. Even as an adult, I still wanted to win the approval of my parents. I wanted them to think I was a successful father. I believed that in their eyes I had failed at everything, and I did not want to fail at being a parent too.

My mother counseled sweetly, "You'd better teach her who's boss right now, or you'll be in big trouble later!" It was the same voice so often used to rationalize the beatings she had inflicted upon me.

As if on cue, I reached out and smashed the child's tiny hand flat on the surface of the table. In that intant I saw the confusion in her eyes turn to hurt and then to pain as they filled with tears. I also saw my parents relax. It was obvious that I had won their approval. But at the expense of my infant daughter.

My parents smiled. I felt sick. I had become like them. Many times since that day I have asked myself why I did not just move the objects out of her reach.

5. *Violence is a deterrent.* Many people believe that violence prevents violence. They suggest that the best way to discipline a child who has just hit another child, for example, is to slap the offender's hand. The thinking behind this action is that if children experience what they are inflicting on others, they will be less inclined to do it again. Also implicit within this approach is the belief that people are less likely to hit others who are ready and willing to hit back. The fear of punishment or retaliation becomes the inhibiting force in these situations.

Perhaps this reasoning would be sound if it were not for one very significant detail: Not all victims of violent attacks are big enough, or strong enough, or old enough to hit back! How many wives are physically strong enough to retaliate against abusive husbands? How many children can defend themselves from attacks of abusive parents? And how many abusive people who hurt their children and spouses are ever really punished by society?

This method may have the desired effect on small children temporarily, but rarely does violence accomplish its ultimate goal. It is a short-term remedy that could have long-term consequences for both the aggressor and the potential victims. Instead of inspiring compliance or obedience, it is more likely to breed anger, resentment, and a desire for revenge that will eventually lead to an attempt at retaliation.

Another problem is that children are given a double message that can be very confusing. The act tells them hitting is acceptable, but the words tell them differently. Which are they to believe? Do actions really speak louder than words?

Violence perpetuates itself. Children who are hit to teach them not to hit will usually be more inclined to use violence to solve their problems. But they will wait until the more powerful adult is not watching or is not around.

I was trying to make this point while speaking to the staff and residents in a school for troubled youth. Most of the young people placed there came from backgrounds of violence and abuse. At the end of my talk, the school administrator came up to speak to me.

"Spanking is the only thing this one kid understands!" he exclaimed emphatically. "Nothing else works!"

"How many times in the last month have you had to spank this boy?" I asked.

77

He paused for a moment to think. "Fourteen," he said at last.

Can you imagine spanking a boy on fourteen different occasions in a month's time?—particularly a boy whose only reason for being there was that he was beaten by his parents? If hitting a boy once does not get the desired result, why would hitting him twice, ten times, or fourteen times be better? It obviously is not working!

Rarely do those who use violence to prevent violence teach or use alternative methods for dealing with conflict. In essence, they do not practice what they preach!

The result? Children learn that it is acceptable for some people to hit some other people. But it is not acceptable for all people to hit all other people. Those who are allowed to hit others must be big and strong enough to get away with it and must be doing it for righteous reasons.

It is acceptable for big people to hit little people and for those in authority to hit those in their care. It is acceptable for parents to hit children, but there are strong prohibitions against children hitting back! It is the age of the victim that determines who can and cannot be legally hit. Under the age of eighteen, young people are appropriate and acceptable targets of adult aggression and hostility.

What do you suppose would have happened if I had tried to defend myself against the abusive attacks of my adoptive parents? Assuming I had survived the attempt, my parents would have had every right to call the juvenile authorities to arrest me for assault. Regardless of provocation, I could have been sent to a juvenile detention center as an incorrigible or placed in a high security center for dangerous adolescents. It is a crime for a child to hit a parent!

Suggesting that violence is a deterrent to violence is a

weak argument. Where is its deterring effect in families where, each year, almost half of all marriages will experience at least one act of spousal violence, and an estimated one million children will be abused?

Violence perpetuates violence, escalates it! This is a truth that has not yet become an acknowledged fact in our culture. Until it does, we will continue treating our social ills with the very poison that is killing us!

The Legacy of Violence

That there is violence in our families is really no surprise. Nor are its destructive effects. In one way or another, we all know it, see it, and suffer because of it. And we also pay for its consequences.

The family is a mirror of society. What is practiced and condoned as acceptable behavior in human relationships at a societal level will be reflected in the family.

Social acceptance of violence in interpersonal relationships—whether as sport or entertainment, to control human behavior or to punish children—is the single most important cause of family violence. Violence rarely occurs in families where there exists a strong prohibition against its use. Just as a nondrinker will never become an alcoholic, a person who never uses violence will never become physically abusive.

Children raised in an environment of violence and abuse tend to grow up believing that human life has little value. Children who are cursed are likely to grow up to curse others. Children who are hit are likely to grow up to hit others. There is a correlation between mothers who hit sons and sons who grow up to hit wives. There is also a correlation between parents who do not have time for their

79

children today and children who will not have time for their parents tomorrow.

Exposure to violence creates a tolerance for violence—not only exposure in the family, but also in the media, particularly television. Every day children witness people being raped and murdered. They are no longer shocked to see human beings attacked, beaten, butchered.

The more we viewers become desensitized to the effects of violence, the more insensitive we become toward its effects on others, and the less likely we are to make an effort to stop or prevent it. People tend to react only to those forces that touch their own lives in some way. The result is that most of us remain mute and uninvolved, seemingly unaware that this life-threatening problem even exists!

To have a winner we can applaud, there must be a loser we can blame. Consider Mr. T and Rambo. What would they be in the eyes of our children if it were not for the victims they overpower?

The legacy of violence and abuse will be passed on to our children . . . unless we stand out of the crowd crying "Crucify him!" and cry out with an even louder "No!" Only when we can choose the ways of Jesus over those of Barabbas will we be able to break the cycle of violence that threatens the health and welfare of us all.

Points to Ponder

1. Why is the American home the most dangerous place in society? What can we do to make it safer?
2. What would happen in your family if you did not allow any use of violence? What would change?

80

3. Is it really necessary to hit children? Are there not other methods of discipline available?

4. Do I tend to glamorize violence? What are my favorite television shows? Are they violent?

5. Am I becoming desensitized to the awful effects of violence? What do I feel when I see it on television?

6. Is hitting a true expression of love? Is that how I want others to express their love for me?

7. Is it acceptable that adults can hit children but children do not have a right to hit back? Is this a double standard?

8. Am I a slave to my ignorance and traditions? Am I really open to new knowledge, new ideas, and new insights?

9. Is violence destroying us? Where does violence rank among the social concerns of our day?

10. Can I prevent the ravages of violence by denying it a place in my life? In my family?

11. Would Jesus suffer the same violent and painful death today?

12. Which do I choose—Jesus or Barabbas? Who will I follow? What will be my destination?

CHAPTER FIVE

Myth 4: *This Is for Your Own Good!*

"What is your name?" my adoptive mother asked as I stood nervously before her and my father.

I was eleven years old. I hesitated before answering, my troubled mind clouded with indecision. Why was she asking my name? Although the question was clear enough, my mother's intentions were not.

Having lived in the adoptive home a year, I had learned there were always hidden expectations behind anything my mother said. Only by discovering the hidden messages and meeting her expectations did I have any hope of pleasing her. It was a game that required the skills of a mind reader.

Lacking those skills, I was not very good at the game. My infantile mind could make no sense of it. This time I was more sure of my answer than of her question. I could not imagine what purpose lay behind it.

But somewhere deep inside, I sensed a trap—the same kind of trap that had snared me before, a trap that had caused me to hurt and bleed. Suddenly frightened, my instinct for survival focused my senses sharply on the woman in front of me.

"My name is Phil," I answered at last, almost as a question.

"No, son, you're wrong!" The intense woman answered me patiently, as though correcting a small child. "Your name is Joe."

This contradiction of what I knew to be true had a visible effect upon me. I knew now that there was a great deal more to her simple question than I could possibly guess. My hands and face twitched uncontrollably from the panic beginning to stir inside me; I lowered my eyes helplessly to the feet of my parents.

I knew I was in trouble. Big trouble! I also knew that I was entirely at the mercy of my parents. If I did not say what they wanted to hear, or do what they wanted me to do, or be what they wanted me to be, I would be punished—just like the other times!

It was not the truth they sought. That was obvious. It was something else. Something of their own design, to be used for their own unfathomable purposes. But what? What was it she wanted me to say? Or was it something she wanted me to do?

I had long ago learned to do or say whatever my parents demanded of me. It was the only chance I had. In my dangerous world there were no such things as right or wrong, good or bad, truth or deceit. Reality was what my parents told me was real. Truth and good and right were what they wanted at the moment. Believing anything else was a threat to my survival.

At the same time I was trying to please my parents by being what they wanted me to be, I had to be careful I was not tricked into saying or doing something that would stir

83

their wrath. They would punish me just as quickly for appearing spineless and giving in to their demands as for resisting them. It was an agonizing struggle to discover in each situation which of the two responses they wanted. A mistake on my part could result in a severe beating.

"Let's try it again," my mother said after a long, tense moment. "What is your name?"

Confused and frightened, I did not know what to answer. If I agreed with her that my name was Joe, then I would be lying. And how many times had I been told that lying would not be tolerated? Lying was a punishable offense. And yet, if I did not agree with her, I took the risk of appearing defiant and contradicting her. That also was an offense sure to bring punishment. What was I to do? I was desperate as the seconds ticked off.

"Your mother asked you a simple question!" It was the harsh, unsympathetic bark of my father. "I suggest you show her the courtesy of answering!" The threat in his impatient voice filled me with the nausea of impending doom.

Although my eyes remained focused on my parents' feet, it was not their feet I was seeing. Unable to resolve the dilemma, my mind sought refuge in other times and other places. Places where I could be alone and untouched by those who would do me harm. Times when I did not have to be so afraid.

But even in my desperate flight into fantasy, I could not escape. Other situations similar to this one flashed mercilessly before my eyes. I could see myself standing before their awful judgment, incapable of meeting their expectations, then suffering the full weight of their disapproval in the punishment that followed. The pain they had inflicted upon my body was almost as severe as the emotional hurt that inevitably accompanied it.

Filled with the familiar horror of a fate I could not change, I knew the same nightmare was beginning again. Even more, I knew there was nothing I could do or say to prevent it. I was trapped. No matter how hard I tried, no matter what I said or did, no matter how much I wanted to please them, it would not be good enough. I would fail. And the penalty for failure was severe.

"For the last time," the woman stated, her voice menacing, "what is your name?"

I knew I had no more time to discover what it was they wanted from me. I would just have to take my chances, answer the question, and hope for the best.

"My name is Phil," I whispered.

"Damn you!" she screamed as she brought her fist down hard on top of my head. "I told you your name was Joe. Are you calling me a liar?"

"No, ma'am!" I pleaded, cowering desperately on hands and knees at her feet. Such a belief in her mind would bring swift and harsh punishment. Softly I began to whimper. "Please don't hurt me!"

"I wouldn't have to hurt you if you weren't so stubborn!" the woman screamed.

It was hopeless! My mother was fast losing control of her anger. The beating was sure to begin soon. That was the way it always happened. Every time. There was no way out.

With a deep sigh of despair, I surrendered my will to the inevitable. Unable to change what was happening, I withdrew deeply into that private inner world I had created for myself. A world where no other could follow; a world beyond the suffering caused by human touch. The

85

only escape left to me now was my own fantasy. And the memory of a dog named Bo. And the sweet, gentle voice of a mother I could hardly remember as she sang, "Jesus loves me, this I know . . . ."

"I'm going to ask you just one more time!" The furious woman slapped me hard across the mouth. "What is your stupid name?"

Looking up through eyes that no longer saw her, I at last said what I thought she wanted to hear. Every part of me was numb and unfeeling.

"Joe," I said.

Teaching Me a Lesson

This is an example of severe emotional abuse. I know there are those of you who will find it hard to believe, just as you found many of the events in *Cry Out!* and *Renegade Saint* hard to believe. It is hard for most of us to believe that adults could do such things to children. But it is even harder for me to forget. It really did occur—unfortunately, more than once.

I do not enjoy remembering such painful experiences. But I believe it is important that I share this event out of my childhood in order to highlight a very important dynamic which was a powerful force in my own family and is usually so in other families where there is violence and abuse.

Like so many parents who unintentionally harm their children, I think my parents really believed that what they were doing was for my own good. They were trying to teach me a lesson—a lesson they thought was very important to my future health and happiness. They really intended to help me become a better person, to build and strengthen my character.

Perhaps I should tell you what happened after I told my mother what I thought she wanted to hear.

After a moment of glaring silence, my parents' anger was gone. Their threats were gone. Their faces cleared and their eyes changed to a lighter hue. Even their voices changed and took on a quality that sounded more like caring, but felt like something else—mockery, perhaps. Or maybe it was their belief that in spite of all the pain, what was happening was a good thing.

Slowly and carefully, they explained to me that what I had just experienced was a designed test of character. They wanted to see if I had the moral courage to stand up for what I knew was right, regardless of the consequences.

Without personal integrity and an unbreakable strength of conviction, they told me, I was sure to fail in the many challenges that would confront me as an adult. It was important that I have backbone, they assured me. Otherwise, I would be no better than the "spineless lowlife" that make up the rank and file of our world. Such people are the scourge of any society. It was their duty as parents to make sure I did not become one of them, and they were prepared to use any means ncessary to accomplish their goal. Adversity, pain, and suffering, they told me, are the building blocks of character!

To their disappointment, I had buckled under the pressure. I had failed the test. I was no better than a worm. It was clear from my poor performance that I had a character flaw that made me vulnerable to peer pressure. It was their responsibility to make sure that flaw was corrected.

I will never forget the words they spoke to me. They were meant as tokens of love but were laced with the poison of self-righteous ignorance.

87

"This is an important lesson you must learn, Phil," they said. "Not only did you tell a bald-face lie—how did you think that you could possibly get away with it?—but you didn't even have the moxie to stand up for what you knew was right. You leave us no choice but to punish you! We'd be negligent in our duty as parents if we let you get away with it. It's the only way you will learn. But it's for your own good!"

I was beaten so severely that I could not get out of bed for two days afterward. The only thing I learned from the lesson was that it would take every ounce of strength I had to survive until I was old enough to get away from them and be on my own.

"I'm doing this for your own good!" How many times did I hear those words while being beaten by my parents during the next several years? How many times do other children hear those words while being beaten and abused? Parents will do almost anything to a child if they believe it is in the child's best interests.

Parenting Intentions

As with most parenting that leaves needless scars on a child, the intentions of my parents were basically good. Most parents want their children to withstand peer pressure and its many lures. There is nothing wrong with wanting children to have a strong character, personal integrity. There is nothing abusive about such a desire. What is damaging is the method they choose to achieve their goal.

My adoptive parents' choice of teaching methods may be attributed to ignorance of the possible short- and long-term effects. In their well-intentioned attempt to fortify my character, their method actually weakened whatever moral strength I might have had and resulted in serious emotional damage that in the long run had an effect opposite to the one they had intended. It did not build character—it destroyed it!

The way we relate to and interact with our children will have a serious impact upon both their present and their future happiness. The lasting effects of what we say and do must never be underestimated.

Nor can we allow ourselves to slip into the belief that commendable results can and must be achieved by whatever means are necessary. The ends do not always justify the means! Yet many people still resort to almost any means to achieve a "good parenting" status, regardless of long-term cost to the child.

Although such people may exist, I have not yet met an abusive parent who intended from the very beginning to hurt, damage, cripple, or destroy a child. In most cases, the parents do love their children, do want what is best for them, and make at least some effort to be good parents.

But good intentions are not enough. If good intentions were all it took to be an effective parent, there would be no abused or hungry children, or children who have no place to live or have been hurt or damaged by adult carelessness. For parents to be effective, those good intentions must be put into good practice. How we parent our children is just as important as why we parent them and the goal we are trying to achieve.

Of what value is it to raise totally obedient children who are afraid to make decisions? Or submissive children with broken spirits? Or responsible children who do not know how to laugh? Or children who think poorly of themselves, or are afraid to love, or afraid of people, life, relationships?

89

Just as the letter of the law may be inhumane unless there is equal regard for the spirit of the law, so too can parenting be abusive without equal regard for the effect on the life of the child. What we do as parents is important. Why we do it is also important. But most important of all is *how* we do it!

Parenting Is Teaching

Everything a parent does involves teaching. We teach children they are wanted by caring for them, providing for their needs, protecting them. We teach them that the world is a wonderful and safe place by providing a home that is wonderful and safe. We teach them the value of human life by the value we place on their lives. We teach them the power of God's love through our love for them. We teach them discipline by disciplining ourselves. We teach important lessons by the things we say and do—as well as by those things we do not say or do.

Expecting from our children what we do not expect of ourselves results in a double standard. We can't expect our children to always tell the truth if they know we lie in situations where to do so is more convenient. We can't expect our children to honor all persons when they hear us constantly berate and criticize those around us. We can't hit our children and expect them to refrain from hitting others.

The old adage that actions speak louder than words is particularly true when dealing with children. Many of us make the mistake of trying to teach our children appropriate behavior by using as our primary teaching tool the same inappropriate behavior we wish to discourage. We hit our children in an effort to teach them not to hit!

90

There is often a fine line between positive learning that teaches "do" and negative learning that teaches "don't," between lessons that reward and those that bring punishment. Children learn best by experiencing the lesson being taught. It is not enough to say, "Don't hit!" They must experience not being hit in order to appreciate the value of not hitting others. The most effective parenting occurs in families that practice what they preach—those that live out the lessons they are trying to teach.

Some lessons do not involve skills that are important for effective living. Instead, they teach values and beliefs. As human beings, we tend to value those things that reflect our beliefs, that confirm what we believe to be true. If we do not believe that honesty is an absolute law that we must strive at all times to keep, we will place little value on it in our relationships, except as it serves our own purposes. The same can be said for loyalty, faithfulness, kindness, peace, or forgiveness.

If we do not believe our parents love us, how can we possibly value God's love for us? If our children cannot experience our forgiveness, how is it possible for them to accept God's forgiveness? Love and forgiveness are truths that exist, but they become real in the lives of our children only as they are experienced. By experiencing them and coming to believe in them, love and forgiveness become building blocks in the foundation of our children's lives.

It is important that we accept and understand our teaching roles as parents. Children must learn certain things in order to live successfully in the family, community, and society. And parents want their children to learn certain things that have to do with beliefs and values. And this is all as it should be. But we must not

91

forget that *how* we teach these important lessons is often as important as the lessons themselves. What value is there, for example, in teaching our children that God loves them if they learn that love is something that hurts or makes them feel guilty?

The issue in parenting is not whether we are "good" or "bad" parents. Such terms are moralistic and infer parental intentions as well as outcomes. Instead, parenting is measured along a continuum of effectiveness. Some parents are more effective than others in achieving their goals. They pay as much attention to how they parent as to what and why they parent. They realize that in the relationship between parents and children, the means are just as important as the ends.

And more often than not, the more effective parents are those who have taken time to learn the skills of parenting. They have altered tradition and overcome ignorance.

The Double Bind

What happened to me is an example of severe emotional abuse. Although most children will never experience emotional abuse to that extent, nor will most parents do such obviously harmful things, there are those who may. Emotional abuse, although one of the most common types of child abuse, is the least recognized and the least reported—and in many cases, the most harmful.

Few life experiences are as potentially damaging to the mental and emotional health of a developing child as the "double bind," a dilemma in which a child is forced to make a choice but will be punished regardless of the choice made. It is a situation in which a child is powerless to avoid punishment.

Double binds result in intense, overwhelming feelings of helplessness and despair on the part of the victim, and such feelings are not the foundation upon which to build mental health, emotional stability, or a happy childhood. Double binds can warp developing personalities, distort thinking, and result in emotional paralysis; they can literally reshape a child's life and destiny.

The double bind in my case is obvious. It did not matter whether I answered that my name was Phil or Joe. I would be punished in either case. There was no way for me to avoid it.

Although not all double binds that confront our children are as severe as those I experienced, all are traumatic and can result in permanent emotional damage. Nor are all parents so blind to the effects of their parenting. What happened to me represents an extreme example of a conflict experienced by many children.

Several years ago I lived in an apartment complex that housed many families with children. I spent a lot of my free time on the grounds of the complex, so I knew most of the kids by name. One of my favorites was Bubba.

Bubba was an average-size child with average athletic ability. But he had the heart of a champion—the determined spirit of a winner. I wondered many times why he had such a strong drive to succeed. Then one day I found out. It was fueled by his fear of disappointing his father.

Some boys were playing basketball, and Bubba's father and several other adults had drifted down to watch the game. Taking a pass from a teammate, Bubba drove hard toward the basket. As he went up for the shot, his elbow caught the bigger boy guarding him on the side of the head. The wounded player lost his temper and hit Bubba,

93

sending him sprawling on the grass. Bubba lay there for a moment, stunned, making no move to retaliate.

After a moment of glaring at each other, the tension eased and the boys prepared to resume the game. It was clear that the boy who had hit Bubba regretted losing his temper and was sorry.

But before Bubba could get to his feet and rejoin the others, his father pulled him up off the ground by one arm, dragged him away a few steps, and began to speak fiercely to him.

"Don't you ever let someone do that to you! If someone hits you, I expect you to hit 'em back! What are you, a man or a worm? Now if you don't get back in there and kick his butt, I'm going to kick yours!"

I watched in dismay as Bubba looked first at the boy who had hit him and then at his father. The pain in his face turned to fear. At last I saw his eyes flood with tears as he set his jaw in fierce determination. Turning slowly, he charged the other boy. The fight was on.

This is a dramatic example of another kind of double bind—threatening to punish a child for losing. Or for not being good enough. Or for not being what we want. Instead of physical punishment, others of us threaten to withhold love or approval or acceptance.

This kind of double bind happens in big ways and little ways, ways we can see and ways that may be hidden from us. But almost always, we believe that what we are doing is for our children's own good.

What happens to the little girl who works for months, with her determined mother driving her, sure that she will win the beauty contest—and then, despite her best efforts, loses? If she wins, she wins her mother's approval, but she also sentences herself to more weeks of grueling rehearsal for the next level of competition. If she loses, she also may lose her mother's approval and is likely to be worked even harder in an effort to overcome the deficiencies that cost her the contest. It is a double bind. In either case, the child loses and will suffer.

Bubba could win his father's approval and avoid being punished only by winning the fight with the other boy. But the other boy was bigger and stronger, and Bubba's chances were slim to none. Not only did he have to take a beating, he had to bear the emotional beating he received from his father when they got home. And as if this were not enough, he also had to bear the punishment he inflicted upon himself for not being good enough to please his father! It was a double bind!

I had a chance to ask Bubba's father about it later. Incensed that I would dare question the reasons for his action, the man assured me it was for the boy's own good.

"I don't want the kid to be a wimp!" he told me seriously. "You know what happens to wimps? The other kids will eat 'em alive, that's what! What kind of father would I be if I let that happen to my son?"

Does that sound familiar? If not, maybe this will:

Her parents and I were still at the dinner table when six-year-old Katie walked through the dining room on her way to the television in the living room. I saw blotches of makeup on her face.

Her mother tensed, then got up and went into the bedroom. After surveying the damage done to the top of her vanity, she returned to the dining room and called Katie.

"Katie, have you been in Mama's makeup again?" she asked, obviously angry.

The child became frightened. Not sure what her mother

would do, she hesitated, shifting from one foot to the other. Her eyes reflected panic.

"No, Mama," she answered at last.

"Don't you lie to me, young lady!" shouted her mother. She took the child by the arms and looked directly into her face. "I'm going to spank you if you do not tell me the truth! Have you been in my makeup?"

"Yes, Mama," the child whispered as she tried to avoid her mother's eyes.

I felt the relief of her parents as the child told the truth. It was obvious that she had been playing where she did not belong. What concerned me was what the mother said next.

"How many times have I told you to leave my makeup alone?"

"Lots," the child answered.

"And what did I say would happen if you got into it again?"

"That you would spank me," the child began to cry.

"I guess you have left me no choice, have you?"

Katie was taken into the bedroom, spanked, and sent to bed. I could hear her sobbing long after her mother returned.

Although the intentions of Katie's mother were good, she had inadvertently put the child in a double bind. Having told Katie that if she ever got into the makeup again she would be spanked, the mother then told her that if she did not tell the truth she would be spanked. The child was going to be spanked whether she told the truth or not! Katie was trapped. There was no way to avoid punishment. It was a no-win situation, a double bind!

Spanking children when they tell the truth is not the way to teach them to be honest. Punishing children when they demonstrate desired behavior discourages them from doing so again. This kind of parenting destroys an honest relationship between parent and child.

Although both Bubba's father and Katie's mother thought they were doing something beneficial, were trying to be good parents, their actions hurt their children more than they helped.

It is not enough for us, as parents, to concern ourselves with the important lessons we must teach our children. *How* we teach them is just as important and can have an even more dramatic impact on the lives of the children.

In the Best Interests of the Child

Generally, the techniques we use to discipline our children are the same as those used by our parents. We use them as expressions of love and concern because our parents did. The belief is that as long as we do it in love, whatever we have done is acceptable.

But hitting a child is *never* an act of love! Many American parents, though, tell us they spank their children because they love them enough to discipline them. Some even believe it is God's will that we hit our children. But above all else, they tell us that spanking works. It accomplishes its purpose. Therefore, they reason, spanking (the means) is justified by the positive result (the end).

Most of these people do not know that it is possible to achieve the same results without hitting their children. Nor do they understand the difference between punishment and discipline. It is not God's will that we hit our children. But he does expect us to *discipline* them. And there is a difference!

97

Nowhere in I Corinthians 13—the great chapter on love—is hitting listed as an act of love. It tells us clearly that love is patient and kind, is never jealous or envious, never boastful or proud, never haughty or selfish or rude. Love is a state of mind, a quality of the spirit that manifests itself in human relationships. Love holds the other person in highest esteem; it does everything possible to uplift the other. Love never hurts; it helps. It never tears down; it builds. Love never punishes; it disciplines!

To equate love with violence is a serious mistake that can have devastating consequences. Love and violence are two entirely different things. If we hit our children because we love them, we must be careful we do not love them to death!

We must care enough about our children to learn to care effectively. The truly Christian approach acknowledges parenting as a very special ministry which requires education, training, and preparation. A child consists of mind, body, heart, and soul, and parents must understand that what affects one part of a child will surely have an effect on the other parts. Parenting must be done from a wholistic perspective, with as much concern for the emotional and spiritual welfare of children as for their physical and mental health.

It is in the best interests of all children when there exists a minimal standard of care and nurturing required of all parents, beyond which we are free to raise our children as we wish. It is in the best interests of children when we understand our relationship to them in terms of stewardship rather than ownership. And it is in the best interests of all children when we reject the ways of Barabbas and choose those of Jesus Christ.

The Gardener

Like many parents overly concerned with how the world will judge their efforts, my adoptive parents spent most of their time and energy looking for what was wrong with me. Their mission was to seek out flaws and correct them. They managed my life as a gardener would a garden— seeking out and destroying the weeds.

But unlike the faithful gardener, rarely did they take time to notice the good fruit! And tragically, they often mistook the new stalk of a plant that would bear good fruit for that of a weed that would bear thorns. In their determined efforts, they trampled the flower in their search for the thorn. The result was a compost pile of tragic human waste, out of which only a divine Creator could bring new life.

Points to Ponder

1. Do I sometimes say and do things to my children I later regret? Things that hurt, rather than help?
2. Do I ever wonder if what I am doing "for their own good" is really in their best interests?
3. Am I willing to learn new parenting techniques in an effort to better myself as a parent?
4. Am I closed to new learning, a slave to traditional ways of doing things?
5. Am I as concerned about the effects of my methods as I am about achieving my parenting goals?
6. Do I believe that hitting my children can be an expression of my love for them? If so, can my children express their love for me in the same way?

7. Do I believe I am free to do anything to my children, as long as I mean them no harm?
8. Do I expect the same from myself as I do my children? Or do I maintain a double standard of conduct in my family?
9. Do I know the difference between discipline and punishment? Do I know the different effects of each on the health and welfare of my children?
10. Do I choose to raise my children in the ways of Barabbas, or in the ways of Jesus?

CHAPTER SIX

Myth 5: *If You Were a Good Parent, You'd Control That Kid!*

Imagine walking into a church on Sunday morning. The building is full of worshipers waiting for the service to begin. We notice two mothers sitting with their toddlers in the pew in front of us.

The mothers are talking together quietly.

The first mother has her arm around a three-year-old child sitting in the pew beside her. The child is not talking, not squirming, not touching, not crying. When the child tries to slip off the pew to play, the mother gently pulls her back and holds her snugly so she cannot move away.

"We must sit still and be quiet in church," she whispers and hands the child a hymnbook to look at. When the child becomes uncomfortable, she begins to whimper. The mother threatens her with a spanking and the child is silent once again.

The second mother also has a three-year-old child. But her child is walking along the length of the unoccupied part of the pew, playing with small toys brought from home. Occasionally the child drops a toy and darts down the aisle a short distance to retrieve it. Bouncing up and down with excitement, he picks up the toy and returns to the pew, chattering softly as he shows it to his mother. She pauses in her conversation to look at what the child is showing her. After a brief discussion about the toy, she cautions the child to speak softly and play quietly so as not to disturb the people around them. The child returns to play while the mother's attention returns to conversation with her neighbor in the pew.

As we observe these two mothers pursuing the same task in the same setting, we are likely to experience different reactions. Whether our reaction is positive or negative, approval or disapproval, it probably is determined by the way we perceive what is happening and how closely it fits with what we think "should" be happening.

The scene with the first mother is what many of us would consider blissfully idyllic! The mother appears to be in control of the situation, the child is "behaving" herself, and the task at hand is being accomplished smoothly and efficiently without disturbance to others. Everything is as it should be, and most of us are likely to express our approval with a warm smile at the child and an appreciative glance at the mother. We judge her a "good mother" because she is in control and the child is under control.

Our response to the second mother is likely to be quite different. That situation appears to be anything but idyllic. Perhaps we feel a mounting anxiety as we watch the pair. The child is unconfined and allowed to move about near his mother. Our discomfort grows as a litany of all the things that could possibly go wrong begin to move through our mind. The child could slip and fall. What an awful scene that would cause! Or he could knock the pile of hymnals off the pew and startle everyone. Or what if he runs into another person coming down the aisle, or trips someone, or is stepped on? He could cause an embarrassing fuss if his will should clash with that of his mother, should she suddenly decide it is time for him to sit still and be quiet. Who knows what an unrestrained child will do next? And who wants the surprise of finding out? Even more important, what must everyone think?

This mother's style of parenting may cause us discomfort. It may not fit nicely into what we think should be happening or what is appropriate behavior for small children in church. Childish behavior in our society is not acceptable anywhere but in nurseries and on playgrounds!

Because we can see only the risks and what is potentially wrong with the situation, we are likely to judge this mother as a "poor parent," or at the very least one who is not doing what she should. Why? Because she appears to be on the verge of being out of control and the child is uncontrolled enough that we fear what he might do next. The mother is not restraining the child enough to suit our own comfort needs; the child's behavior is a *distraction*. The kid is being a *nuisance!*

Good Parents Control Their Children

We judge the first mother to be a good parent. The second mother does not fare so well. Why? Because the first meets our own standard of what it means to be a good parent, and the other does not. At the very least we would call her permissive. Good parents control their kids. Or so we think, because that is what we have been told!

What is most striking to me in this situation is not whether the two mothers are good or bad parents, whether they are in control of their children or not, or even whether they meet my personal standards of good parenting. Most

103

interesting, and also my greatest concern, are the two children. Which of the two is the more normal child?

Something may be wrong with a child who sits so passively beside the mother during a long service. Physical and emotional passivity are not typical of healthy, normal, three-year-old children.

By developmental standards, the more normal child is the one who is actively communicating with his mother, actively pursuing his curiosity up and down the length of the pew, actively engaged physically, mentally, and emotionally in what is happening around him. This child is involved, alive, experiencing, learning, growing. The child is active!

And yet these are the very same qualities we find so distressful and believe we must discourage in our children if they are to be "well behaved." The very definition of what it means to be a good parent in our society is in conflict with normal child development. The result is that we punish our children for being normal! And what will happen if we punish them for being normal? It is likely that we will raise abnormal children!

Though inconvenient at times, we all would do well to encourage and seek to develop these normal, active, positive qualities in our children. Often, they are the difference between high and low achievers; happy and unhappy children; children who are able to maintain a level of personal satisfaction and success, and those who suffer from low self-esteem and the debilitating feelings of personal inadequacy.

I am not saying that children should be totally unrestrained. Not at all! Of course there must be limits, but limits designed to teach and protect, not enslave or imprison; limits that foster growth and learning, not inhibit it.

We do not want to raise passive children. Passive people become victims, easy targets of exploitation and abuse. Pedophiles, for example—adults who sexually exploit children—can pick out likely targets on a playground after only a few moments. They look for children who appear detached, alone, passive, vulnerable.

On the other hand, we do not want to raise aggressive children who abuse or exploit others. The goal of effective parenting is to raise assertive children—children who can express themselves, fulfill themselves, protect themselves, and achieve a level of personal success within reasonable, socially acceptable limits.

The tragedy for many children, however, is that some parents are so concerned about socially accepted standards that they hear only the voices that tell them to control their kids—the voices of society, the voices of the police, the voices of the schools, the voices of the neighbors, even the voices of their own family members—telling them to control their kids.

In their desperate effort to be good parents, they may find themselves saying and doing things to their children they would never dream of doing or saying to another human being. They may become confused and forget that *how* they parent is as important as *what* they parent. They may even discover the most powerful tool available for controlling another human being—pain.

Violence works. It is the quickest, most accessible, and most effective means of control. And it requires no special training or education. But the effect of violence on behavior is generally short-term. Like a drug, it wears off. Then it must be administered again, and this time it will take a little longer to achieve the same temporary result.

But there are long-term consequences as well, for both

105

child and parent. Parents who measure their success by how well they control their children tend to become dominating. They enforce the letter of the law with no thought for the spirit behind it. The children are enslaved to their parents' expectations much as the parents are in bondage to the expectations of others. Their concern is that they be the kind of parents they believe society demands.

Such was the case with my adoptive parents. Desperate to be "good" parents, they would do almost anything not to fail in the eyes of those whose approval they sought most. In their minds, being a parent was the one area of human activity in which no one should fail. As a result of this kind of thinking, they were determined to establish and maintain absolute control. The means were unimportant. Their success would be measured by the end result, they reasoned, not the unfinished product. Besides, it was all for my own good. The pain would make me a better man. The suffering would build character. (Assuming, of course, that I survived!)

My parents discovered what most abusive parents discover: Violence works! We *can* control the behavior of children with violence—until they are old enough and strong enough to hit back; as long as we are in the same room; or until our back is turned.

But there is a price to pay for the use of violence in our most intimate and precious relationships. It is a price we all must pay in terms of human suffering as well as tax dollars—the price of tyranny.

Controlling Parents

My adoptive father was an ex-military man, physically intimidating, and his style of parenting was militaristic. Coming from a situation in which even a moment's hesitation in obeying an order could cost not only his life but the lives of others, he insisted upon total, unquestioned obedience.

My adoptive mother, on the other hand, had been the youngest of nine children in a puritanical, patriarchal family in which there were only three females. I suspect she grew up resenting male control and the way that control was exercised. She was dominated by persons older, bigger, and stronger, all of whom knew what was best for her.

Control of themselves and the people around them were important concerns for my adoptive parents. This is easy to understand when we remember the life situations out of which they came. Loss of control means personal vulnerability, something neither of them could handle. And it is understandable that this need for control would be extended to their adopted children. Believing themselves totally responsible for the way I might turn out, they demanded total control, complete submission, unquestioned obedience, and no interference.

Is it any wonder abuse evolved? They were set up to fail as parents from the very beginning—set up by society's definition of good parenting, by their own desperate need to win social approval and acceptance, and by their own experience of childhood. Because of tradition and ignorance, my adoptive parents were set up to fail, and I was set up to suffer through an unimaginable hell.

They became tyrannical parents, and our relationship, my childhood, and any hope of an adult life free of infantile terrors—all were sacrificed to human madness on the altar of righteous punishment for my own good!

Controlling parents tend to share similar characteristics:

1. *Obedience is demanded.* Such parents insist upon strict obedience at all times. Their authority and their decisions are not to be challenged. Challenges are seen as threats and must be dealt with accordingly if family unity is to be preserved. There is no greater crime in such families than disobedience, and punishment must be harsh and quick. Compliance and submission to the will of the parents are valued above all else as essential character-building qualities. Love and rewards are given only as long as children are obedient.

2. *Expectations are unrealistic.* Controlling parents tend to expect a very great deal from their children, and many of those expectations are beyond the children's capacity. They include not only how the children function within the family but their performance outside it as well, and failure to meet these expectations is often viewed as disobedience.

3. *Children are viewed as little adults.* These parents have little knowledge of child development and what can be expected of children in terms of thinking and behavior at particular ages. Childhood misbehavior is often attributed to complex adult motives, intentional challenges to parental authority.

I frequently show a film called "Suffer the Children, Silence No More" when I speak on child abuse before medical professionals. The opening scene shows a young mother sitting in her living room while her baby is crying in a crib across the room. She is obviously frustrated and in great distress. She has done everything she can think of to get the infant to stop crying, but nothing has worked, and at last she can stand it no longer.

She rushes angrily across the room and screams at the child, "If you loved me, you'd stop crying!"

But this only frightens the baby and it screams more

loudly. The mother has begun to ascribe adult thinking and motivation to the infant. She believes the baby is crying on purpose.

More often than not, children's intentions are perceived to be malicious, designed to hurt, reject, or get even with the parent. It is not that children *cannot* do what is expected, it is that they *refuse* to do so. These parents view misbehavior as a willful choice that represents rebellion against parental authority. Feeling wronged, these parents are likely to withdraw emotionally from their children and neglect their needs or lash out in angry retaliation. In either case, the children are made to suffer.

4. *These parents rule by rules.* Controlling parents tend to have rules for everything. Even simple tasks have hard and fast procedures that must be followed if they are to be done "right." All aspects of human living fall into a clear category of right or wrong; there are no gray areas of ambiguity or uncertainty. It is all or nothing, for me or against me, good or bad—a life-style of extremes.

Very religious parents often add all the rules of their religion to their own rules. When this happens, submission to parents can be confused with submission to God. The children learn that obedience to parents, or to any authority figure, is also obedience to God. Such teaching can be very dangerous! It can lead to blind faith in a fanatic cult. It can also motivate a conscientious Christian woman to submit to the authority of a battering husband until it is too late for both of them.

Children who are obedient and submissive are good. Those who are not are bad. The good child is loved, wanted, valued, rewarded. The bad child is rejected and punished. Never is there a distinction made between a child and the child's behavior; it is not the behavior that is bad and deserving of punishment—it is the child!

Rules become the masters of life and must be obeyed at all cost. They are even more important than the lives they control.

5. *Mistakes are viewed as crimes.* Mistakes are as much a part of learning as is repetition. Little learning would occur without mistakes, and success is most often achieved through repeated failures. Yet the domineering parent tends to view normal, predictable childhood mistakes as crimes, committed most often willfully and with malicious intent.

In our society, crimes are to be punished, and the reprisals inflicted by these parents are often harsh and extreme, viewed as just punishment. Tragically, these children carry the record of their "crimes" with them for the rest of their lives. Crimes are never forgiven, and the burden for the child can be a lifetime of guilt—guilt for being human.

6. *Control is achieved through fear and intimidation.* The primary feature of controlling parents is that they tend to be authoritarian and autocratic. They rule with strict discipline and accountability. They tolerate no opposition and rely heavily on physical and emotional intimidation. These parents may use threatened or actual force, or they may use guilt and shame, but with equal effect.

They often play the role of the proud patriarch or matriarch and give the public impression that everything is under control. They go to great lengths to hide any problems at home and preserve their image of competence.

Family members are likely to be gratefully dependent upon such persons, and the parents often see other family members as being in their debt, owing them obedience and anything else they might demand. In extreme cases, this might even include sexual favors.

The typical mode of family interaction is designed not to bring closeness, but efficiency; not to inspire joy and laughter, but fear and obedience; not to encourage the growth and development of all members, but to service the needs of the parents and preserve the family as a unit at all costs.

Controlling people generally fear closeness to others and hide their need for intimacy behind either macho or martyr attitudes. Many do not know how to become emotionally intimate with others. They have few if any close friends and tend to fill their lives with "things"—rules and power—as substitutes for the intimacy they so desperately desire, yet fear. These parents do great emotional harm to their developing children; they make possible only one type of relationship within the family—master and servant.

7. *They confuse discipline with punishment.* These parents generally do not know the difference between discipline and punishment. The purpose of discipline, they believe, is to direct the thoughts and control the actions of their children. Punishment is a way to control behavior. Therefore, they reason, punishment *is* discipline.

Nothing could be further from the truth! The goal of discipline is not to control, but to teach appropriate and acceptable behavior, to teach children to control themselves!

Punishment, in one way or another, always tears children down at an emotional level. But discipline builds them up, makes them more confident, more sure of themselves and the world around them. Discipline does not inflict pain or inspire fear. It bestows love and inspires confidence. It is one thing to inspire conformity in our children and quite another to beat them into submission. That is the difference between discipline and punishment.

111

My youngest daughter has a playmate named Tommy. They spend a great deal of time together and are good friends. Yet, like all three-year-olds, they have occasional conflicts.

Early in their relationship, Morgan's mother saw her hit Tommy because he would not let her have a toy she wanted. Her mother had three choices: She could ignore the incident and hope it would not happen again; she could punish Morgan for "committing a crime"; or she could discipline her for making the mistake of using hitting as a way to get what she wanted.

Her mother reasoned that ignoring what happened would only guarantee that it would occur again in a similar situation. She decided that hitting the child for hitting Tommy was not the answer. She chose, instead, to discipline her. Now, discipline involves a series of teachings:

1. Point out the mistake: hitting to get what is wanted.
2. Tell the harmful effects: It hurts Tommy and makes him unhappy. It also makes him want to hit back!
3. Discuss alternative methods of handling the situation: Ask Tommy for the toy, wait until he is finished, or find a similar toy.
4. Motivate toward reconciliation: Apologize and share a hug with Tommy.

Morgan learned that she does not have a right to hit anyone, nor does anyone have a right to hit her.

Because her mother chose to use discipline rather than punishment, and knew how to use it, Morgan did not walk away from that experience a "criminal," a bad person. Instead, she enjoyed the playtime and also began to learn some important lessons about handling conflict and solving problems. But most important, she felt warm and secure in the love of a mother she could trust to help, rather than judge in ways that would hurt.

Perpetual Victims

Children who are unable to win their parents' approval and acceptance or achieve parental standards of thought and conduct will soon reach a point where they no longer even try. They learn it is safer to make no effort at all than to try and fail, and then feel guilty for not being good enough.

From my own abusive childhood, I learned that in order to survive, I had to keep people from expecting too much. The root of all disappointment is expectation, so as long as I allowed people to expect good things, I ran the risk of disappointing them. Failing to meet other people's expectations always made me feel guilty, and I felt that if I took on enough guilt, sooner or later it would drive me to suicide. I learned I could live with rejection, so I had to make sure no one expected anything good from me. That way I could not fail! And there was no way I could live with guilt.

Children who feel guilty about not being good enough, or who in their own minds always fail, tend eventually to give up on themselves and on life. They become perpetual victims who live according to chance, fate, luck. Nothing happens in their lives because they make it happen, but only by some act of a will greater than their own. Such a perception of the world and one's place in it is nothing less than an emotional disability.

These children must learn it is OK to make mistakes, that mistakes do not make them bad persons or failures. Mistakes are opportunities for parents to exercise discipline and for children to learn. Mistakes are not crimes. They are the growing edge of healthy, well-adjusted children on their way to healthy, well-adjusted adulthood.

Learned Disability

In another form of overcontrol, parents insist upon making all decisions for their children. Some parents continue to pick out their children's clothes, their food, their friends, and even tell them how to spend their free time. These parents maintain total control, refusing to allow their children the freedom to make some of their own choices.

Children learn to make sound decisions by making choices and experiencing the effects of those choices. Without this opportunity, they do not develop the sense of self-control, self-confidence, and competence so necessary for healthy development.

Parents who treat their children as invalids will raise persons incapable of caring for themselves or making their own decisions. They tend to grow up looking for someone to control their lives and make their decisions for them. Such uncertainty and inadequacy represent a serious emotional handicap.

There are also parents who believe it is their duty to tell their children not only what to do, but how to do it. Children do not learn competence through constant instruction or having things done for them. They must eventually be allowed to do things themselves—to succeed or fail. It is the attempt, the trying, that is most important in learning. Children who are never allowed to pull themselves to their feet will never learn to stand alone and walk.

The constant discouragement of assertiveness or punishment of attempts at self-control, self-determination, and self-expression can result in learned disability—the

114

inability to attempt at all! Often the difference between ability and disability is the parent's permission to try and perhaps fail.

Implied Threat

Indicative of a tyrannical approach to parenting is the statement that ends with an obviously implied threat of punishment, should the child fail or not comply.

Tyrants maintain their authority and control by the threat or actual use of force. Or-else statements instill fear; they deny the right of self-determination, the right to make one's own choices. It takes an act out of the "want to" category and places it firmly in the "have to" category. Rarely are children as enthusiastic about, nor do they benefit as much from "have to" situations as from those they desire for themselves. Nothing is more certain in such instances than that children's resentment will build and resistance will result. Most damaging of all, as parents continue to force their will upon their children, parents and children are placed in adversary roles. Rather than a cooperative effort, the relationship becomes a power struggle—a battle of wills and there can be no real winner.

Closed-Mind Parenting

Controlling parents tend to discourage or forbid dicussion of new ideas or new ways of doing things. They are most secure and have the greatest control as long as attitudes, beliefs, and ways of doing things remain the same. Change is threatening because it may challenge their hold on the family, so their minds are closed, unwilling to consider or allow even the possibility of anything new and different.

115

Such conditions breed passivity, resentment, anxiety, disinterest, apathy.

There is no right of appeal in such families; every decision is final. There are no alternatives; everything is clear and precise, with no room for discussion or debate. As a result, the entire family revolves around the moods of the person who possesses the power. All others are subservient. Reality is what the parent says it is. Individual thought is discouraged and punished; free thinking is not conducive to compliance.

Such home environments tend to be stagnant, uninformed, a breeding ground for myth and misperception upon which the children must base their understanding of reality. This, too, can result in emotional problems. Such inflexibility of thought, rigidity of belief, and extremely limited vision cannot help affecting children in undesirable ways.

Double Standards

Although controlling people tend to impose law, they are above the law. Certain behaviors prohibited in their children are overlooked in themselves.

This double standard of human conduct teaches children that it is not certain behavior that is unacceptable, but simply their age and size. Children are forbidden to do certain things that adults are allowed to do. It becomes a matter, then, of waiting until they are old enough and big enough.

The expression of anger is a good example. Most parents prohibit open and physical displays of temper in their children. Such exhibitions often bring swift punishment. Yet parents rarely impose similar restraints upon their own emotions. Many parents do not hesitate to punish their children while in a rage. Freely expressed and often violent parental anger is not uncommon.

Such a double standard is of little concern to controlling parents; they do not want to be imitated, only obeyed. Their approach is based on "Do as I say, not as I do!" But the result contradicts everything the parent is trying to teach, since it is the parents' behavioral model, not their words, that will have the greatest impact on the developing child. Children do imitate their parents. And abusive parents tend to raise abusive children.

Control is the critical issue for parents who exercise a style of parenting that demands absolute obedience. They tend to control every area of their children's lives—their activities, home environment, thinking, behavior. Obedience is the most prized quality in their children.

These families are riddled with rules—lots of rules—and violation of the rules is a serious offense, which usually requires punishment. Families in which there exist more "can'ts" than "cans" create a dreary prison of restrained childhood.

The Really Good Parents Are Effective Parents

Almost anybody can be a "good" parent. But not everybody can be an effective parent. With few exceptions, every parent I have met has qualified as a good parent. Even my own adoptive parents were good parents—at least in the beginning. They were concerned, they provided the basic life necessities, and their parenting techniques differed from those used by most parents only in that they were extreme. Their intentions were noble, and they kept me under control. But were they successful parents?

117

Successful parents are measured not by their intentions, but by their effectiveness. They know what they want to achieve, and they use effective techniques for achieving those goals. Successful parents are knowledgeable people who make the time and effort necessary to learn about effective parenting before they become parents. They are not nearly as concerned about what the neighbors might think as they are about the health and welfare of their children.

By modern standards, good parents control their children. Effective parents, on the other hand, teach their children to control themselves. The first use punishment; the other, discipline. As a result, some children can rightly be called well-disciplined, while others are more accurately described as well-punished. We usually can tell the difference between well-punished children and well-disciplined children by what they do when we leave the room! The first will go wild, exploiting the absence of their external source of control, while the others will continue to exercise self-control. There is a no more undisciplined child than the well-punished child!

Points to Ponder

1. What does being a "good" parent mean to me? Does it mean I must control my children at all times?
2. If my responsibility as a parent is to control my children, am I free to use any means necessary to accomplish that goal?
3. Do I understand the difference between discipline and punishment? Which do I use with my children?

4. Can I think of times I may have punished my children for being normal—for behaving in ways appropriate to their age?
5. Am I raising a passive child? An aggressive child? Do I know the difference between aggressiveness and assertiveness?
6. How do I measure my success as a parent? Am I overly concerned with what others might think?
7. Do I have realistic expectations of my children? Do I sometimes expect them to act and think like little adults?
8. Do I perceive childhood mistakes as crimes? Do I try to find a punishment to fit the crime?
9. Do I maintain a double standard of conduct for myself and my children? Do I expect more of them than of myself?
10. If given a choice, would I rather be a "good" parent or an "effective" parent? What is the difference?

CHAPTER SEVEN

Myth 6: *I Can Raise My Kid Any Way I See Fit!*

It took several days to make the long drive, with only an occasional rest stop during the daylight hours. Two adults in the front seat and three near-adolescent males in the back meant there was not much room for stretching cramped legs or shifting tired bodies into more comfortable positions. The heat of the Arizona desert was suffocating, stifling all conversation between my adoptive parents. Hungry, thirsty, and miserable most of the time, I gazed blindly out the window as one endless mile after another appeared to draw us no closer to the skyline. Like almost everything else in my life, I wondered if it would ever be over.

We were on a two-week vacation to visit relatives in Southern California. I was thirteen.

We stopped each night only when dusk fell upon us like a blanket and the fatigue of being locked up in a moving vehicle for so long threatened to overpower us. Turning off the highway, we would grope our way blindly through campgrounds along a road already filled with other weary travelers, until at last we found a vacant site. Then, with

120

tempers flaring and much cursing, I would flounder wildly in the darkness to help set up camp under the critical and often punishing supervision of my parents. Any difficulty I had unscrewing and adjusting the rusty tent poles or driving stakes into the rocky ground would invariably bring a barrage of curses, along with a blow to the head or a hard-soled boot against my backside.

By the time supper was prepared, I would be so upset I could hardly eat. But I dared not show it for fear of inciting their anger. I had learned much earlier that my survival depended on not attracting their attention; it took little enough as it was to bring down their wrath.

Camping with my adoptive parents was a miserable ordeal. It hurt. Traveling with them, being in the same small space for such a long time, just being in the same world with them—it all hurt. Physically and emotionally. If there is a hell, I know it well!

To withstand my vulnerability while confined with my parents for so long, I withdrew so completely inside myself that I would respond only when necessary to avoid punishment. Keeping aloof and at a great emotional distance from everyone around me was my only defense against being overwhelmed by my inability to be what my parents expected me to be. Apathy and passivity can provide a protective shield.

The entire family was exhausted by the time we arrived at my uncle's house. Then matters only became worse. My adoptive parents wanted me to be a model adolescent—an all-American boy who would bring them great honor and praise. They expected me to be alert, courteous, and obedient, the epitome of good parenting. What they wanted was a happy, well-adjusted young man.

What they got was something quite different. I was shy,

fearful, withdrawn, depressed. The result was a growing hostility, in addition to their already festering anger and resentment at being trapped in an adoption with a child they no longer wanted.

It took only a couple of days for that anger to spill over into action. They took me into the bedroom and shut the door. They accused me of being disrespectful and rude to my uncle's family. My depression was interpreted as sullen insolence, my withdrawal as arrogant indifference, my natural shyness as willful lack of cooperation designed to make them look bad in the eyes of their family. Such an attitude would no longer be tolerated, they said. They were going to give me the "spanking" I deserved.

At their instruction, I dropped my pants and underwear and bent over the bed, and the blows began, at first mild and well spaced. But I could sense the growing intensity with each blow—an intensity I had experienced so many times before. Again and again the belt slapped against my bare buttocks.

Soon the blows came faster and faster, with more force. I could feel the rage building as my parents began to lose control. After my mother tired, my father took over. I could feel blood beginning to trickle down my legs. Then the blows moved from my buttocks to my legs and back. Again and again he struck, in a frenzy of unrestrained violence.

When at last my legs buckled, so bruised they could no longer hold my weight, my father grabbed my hair and held me upright while my mother used the belt again. In her rage she turned it around so that the buckle struck me.

I could feel consciousness slipping away when the bedroom door burst open. It was clear even to me that my uncle was frightened and upset. His face was bloodless and though he avoided looking at me, I could see through the pained glaze over my own eyes that his were brimming with tears.

"For heaven's sake, stop it!" he yelled. "That kid's going to get up in the night and try to kill you!"

The blows stopped. My parents seemed stunned that anyone would dare interfere. An awful silence followed the abrupt intrusion, broken only by my parents' heavy breathing. The electric tension in the room began to ease.

I watched with the desperation of a trapped animal as my parents visibly relaxed. It was almost as though they were waking from a dream—a nightmare from which it would take me weeks to recover.

At last my mother laid the belt aside and approached her brother. She was smiling now; her features were no longer etched in the granite of righteous violence.

"Now, Harry, we're only doing what we have to do," she explained calmly. "Do you think we like having to spank a thirteen-year-old boy who should know better?"

"But this?" he asked, his voice still strained.

"You don't know him, Harry! We have to come down hard on him. It's the only thing he understands. It's for his own good!"

"But Sis—" he tried to protest.

"This is no concern of yours, Harry!" my mother cut him off, her voice now stern and uncompromising. "I know what you are trying to do, and I appreciate it. But you are wrong. Dead wrong! We have a right to raise our children as we see fit! And you have no right to interfere!"

My uncle left the room without another word, taking with him that faint glimmer of hope he had brought when he entered, leaving in its wake an even deeper despair. His withdrawal only reaffirmed what my parents had been telling me since the first time they hit me: I deserved the punishment they inflicted. It was my fault they had to be so mean and brutal. And they were doing it because they loved me!

The tension that resulted from this incident drove the families apart. Although nothing more was said, I could tell my uncle did not approve, but this awareness was no comfort to me. I had no illusions of rescue. I reasoned that he would have approved if he had known I was as bad as my parents said.

We left after only another day. I was punished again and again for ruining the family vacation and disturbing my mother's relationship with her brother. Everything was my fault.

I was an emotional wreck by the time we returned home. Even more tragic, I wished I were dead.

Discipline? Or Abuse?

Only a small minority of parents intentionally harm their children, but those people are the perpetrators of the severe cases of child abuse. The most common child abusers, however, are the well-intentioned parents who use techniques that are potentially damaging.

Desperate, damaged adults are more likely to maltreat their children than are those who had healthy childhoods in well-adjusted families. I suspect that both my adoptive parents grew up in families that condoned harsh physical punishment for childhood misbehavior. While this does not excuse their actions, it does make them more comprehensible. We know that parenting is largely a skill learned by watching our own parents.

There can be little doubt that what my parents did was

not discipline. It was punishment—harsh, cruel punishment!

The word *discipline* comes from a Latin word which means *to teach.* It does not mean *to hit, to push, to shove,* or *to force.* Many studies have been done on the most effective methods of teaching, and hitting has never been identified as an effective method. On the contrary, it has been shown to inhibit learning!

The willful infliction of pain and suffering is called *abuse.* A mild form of abuse used for revenge, retribution, or as a way to control the behavior of children is called corporal punishment. Its goal is not to teach, but to control. Fear, force, and pain are the least effective teaching methods available and are the most damaging to the developing personality of the child.

The effect of that kind of punishment motivates children to survive by being and doing and saying whatever is necessary to avoid subsequent beatings. Truth or lie, good or bad, right or wrong no longer exist for them. The only other effect of such beatings is to deepen children's distrust of and alienation from their parents.

The actions of my parents only added more fuel to an already simmering rage, a rage that eventually would result in the suffering of many people—innocent victims who had done nothing to hurt me. It would also lead to my decision to try to kill my adoptive parents as the only possible means of escape from that hell of being systematically destroyed by the very people upon whom I must depend.

It is true that most child abuse is not as severe as that I experienced. But it is also true that almost every severe case of child abuse that leaves a child permanently scarred and damaged—or dead—began years before as "spankings" and mild abuse. At that time it was treatable and more severe abuse was preventable. There was hope for both the child and the family. But by the time the case comes to the attention of professionals who can help child and parents, it is too late. The damage is done.

It is difficult sometimes to know if what we are doing or saying to our children is helping or hurting them; whether it is truly discipline or an early, mild form of punishment that can lead to severe child abuse. Perhaps the following criteria will help parents to better judge the immediate and long-term effects of parenting techniques:

1. *Abuse tends to be a pattern of hurtful behavior.* Although it is possible for a single interaction between a parent and child to be abusive, as in the case of severe physical attack or rape, most child abuse tends to be a parental or care-giver pattern of behavior that has a negative effect on the child. It causes physical, mental, emotional, or spiritual suffering or injury.

The goal of effective parenting is not to hurt our children, but to help them. Actions such as those of my parents hurt physically by leaving bruises, cuts, and welts. They hurt emotionally by fueling resentment and hatred. They hurt mentally by teaching a child to distrust and fear intimate contact with other human beings. They hurt spiritually by causing a child to confuse love and violence, teaching that violence is an acceptable expression of love.

2. *The effect of the maltreatment is observable.* The kind of parent/child interaction that is of the greatest concern is not that which hurts so much as that which damages. All parents say and do things to hurt their children, but those hurts can heal. Damage never heals. Whether it results in a physical scar, a mental problem, or an emotional

handicap, the effect of maltreatment usually can be observed in a child's abnormal appearance, performance, functioning, or behavior. Sexual abuse will usually affect the way a child relates to adults and to peers.

There can be no doubt that my parents damaged me. And that damage became apparent in the way I thought, the feelings I expressed, the way I behaved. Survival behavior, adaptive thinking, and aggressive feelings are not characteristics of healthy, well-adjusted children. They tend to inhibit growth and development.

There are instances, however, in which the effect of maltreatment will not become observable until it surfaces as dysfunction in adulthood. An example of this might be the gradual, unnoticed erosion of a person's self-esteem.

3. *The effect of the maltreatment is not temporary.* The physical effects of some types of child abuse can be temporary. Unless damaged beyond repair, the body has an incredible healing capability. But the heart, mind, and soul may not heal so quickly or so completely. It is the unobserved, nonphysical effects that tend to be most long lasting. They can lie repressed in the personality for many years, only to surface later in life as serious psychopathology that may threaten the child's welfare, the welfare of the child's family, or perhaps even the welfare of innocent victims on the street.

Maltreatment brings about an erosion of a child's capacity to think, feel, believe, and function. There should not be a price tag on childhood. But thousands of people must pay that price every day for the rest of their lives.

4. *The effect of the maltreatment consitutes a handicap for the child.* Anything that makes becoming a well-adjusted adult more difficult can be considered a handicap—a physical, mental, emotional, or spiritual condition

127

that interferes with healthy growth, development, and functioning. It results in an impairment of the ability to think, feel, learn, and enter into healthy, satisfying relationships with others.

Identifying the Emotionally Abused Child

Experts in the fields of child development and mental health agree that physical and emotional abuse can be devastating to a child and can cause serious problems in adulthood. Without hesitation, these professionals admit that abuse does occur, and with alarming frequency. It represents a powerful force that shapes the lives and personalities of thousands of children every day. We can describe child abuse and provide countless examples. We can talk about it, write about it, even treat it. But we cannot define it!

Since the 93rd Congress passed the Model Child Abuse Prevention and Treatment Act in 1974, many attempts have been made to arrive at a comprehensive, legal definition of child abuse. But thus far, all have failed or proven inadequate.

The public generally thinks of child abuse solely in physical terms, with little awareness of the impact of emotional assault and deprivation on the overall health and development of a child. These dangers are not commonly known outside mental-health circles, partly because, unlike physical wounds, emotional wounds often remain hidden for years, perhaps even a lifetime—always there, always felt, but never seen. Yet those wounds are just as real, just as painful and can have a similar or even greater effect on a child.

Current laws are concerned primarily with acts of commission or omission which have a clear causal link between parental behavior and physical harm or possible harm to the child. They make no provision for emotional consequences, yet the evidence concerning emotional abuse is clear. It tends to affect a child's ability to learn and function successfully within socially acceptable limits. And if severe enough, it can alter the course of a child's life, often with tragic consequences.

It is difficult sometimes to tell whether a child is being emotionally maltreated or suffering from an emotional disturbance caused by something else. Often the behavior of both emotionally disturbed and emotionally abused children is similar. In such instances, it may be helpful to look at the responses of the parents to help determine which is more likely the case.

Parents of the emotionally disturbed child tend to accept the existence of the problem, are concerned about the child's immediate and long-term welfare, and are actively involved in seeking help for the child. Parents of the emotionally abused child, however, tend to ignore the problem or deny that it exists, may blame the child for the problem, are likely to refuse offers of help, are generally unconcerned about the child's welfare, and tend to resent intervention. Which of these two responses better characterized my adoptive parents?

Child Protection and Parental Rights

Throughout recorded history parents have had absolute power and authority over their children. This generally has been understood as a parental right—the right to raise children by family standards, without state intervention or control.

In earlier times children were regarded as pieces of property with economic value. This medieval concept of parental "ownership" is reflected in contemporary family relationships when children are referred to as "belonging" to their parents.

The ancient Roman doctrine of *patria potestas* endowed the Roman head of household with the same power over his offspring as over his livestock and material possessions. This doctrine also united the two acts of will—the act of creating and the act of destroying. As a result, children—like other pieces of property—could be bought and sold, beaten, molested, mutilated, or destroyed.

With their value measured in economic terms, many children served the needs of their families by working as prostitutes, circus attractions, or beggars. In the latter two instances, it was clear that the more grotesque a disfigurement, the more sympathy the children would elicit from spectators and passers-by, and the more profitable they would be. Intentional disfigurement of children was a common practice in those families.

As the archaic concept of parental ownership is clearly reflected in modern societies, so too is the concept of parents' inherent right to destroy that which they have created. Even today, the natural "right to life" of all children continues to be in serious doubt and is a controversial issue.

In addition, beatings and other forms of severe punishment were believed necessary to drive out evil spirits and control a child's behavior in order to ensure good character development and eventual acceptance into society. Religious teachings, social customs, and traditional beliefs supported these practices as a parental right or, in some cases, duty.

Even today abusive parents tend to appeal to the highest ideals of love, duty, and parental rights as justification for abuse of their children. Some of the most severe examples of physical, emotional, and sexual abuse are rationalized on righteous grounds. Though such rationalizations may ease consciences, they do not alter the painful reality or the devastating consequences.

The Middle Ages witnessed the conception of the doctrine of *parens patriae*, which recognized that parental rights brought corresponding responsibilities. The right to bear a child brought with it the responsibility to care for that child by providing basic needs.

The Supreme Court of the United States has recognized and defended the right of the individual to initiate and preserve an autonomous private family, with strictly limited government interference. Recognizing that society is built upon strong, stable, healthy families and that the family is better suited than the state to raise children, traditional governmental policy has been to secure parental rights as necessary for the maintenance of families—often at the expense of the children. Not nearly as much attention has been given by the Court to parental responsibilities to provide at least a minimal standard of care and nurturing to the children they have a right to bear and raise.

Acknowledging that parents have certain responsibilities gave birth to the concept that the child has a right to expect those responsibilities to be fulfilled. The birth of "child rights" as a legitimate concern of public policy sparked new demands that the rights of all individuals, regardless of age, sex, race, or religion, be protected through equality under the law. And modern history has witnessed a dramatic struggle to see this ideal realized.

Along with the acknowledgment that children do have certain rights came an awareness of the state's responsibility to protect those rights by direct intervention in the family if necessary. Apart from the protection of individual rights, justification of state intervention was based on its interest in the health and welfare of its children—not only because its future depends on them, but because the state must assume responsibility for the problems inflicted upon society as mistreated children grow into maladjusted adults.

The evolution of "minimal care" standards as a responsibility of parents, and the state's responsibility to intervene on behalf of children not receiving that care, has been a slow process characterized by profound resistance and great social controversy. Legislation to protect the rights of children is more difficult to achieve than legislation to guarantee the rights of adults. The expansion of child rights invariably means that lawmakers must cross over into domestic territory and is certain to be misinterpreted by some as an attack on the traditional family.

Since the feudal period, the state has recognized its responsibility to protect citizens not capable of protecting themselves, but most reform legislation has been directed at providing protection outside the home. There continues to be great reluctance to provide similar protection within the family, despite current statistics that identify the home as the most dangerous place in society.

The struggle to attain a healthy balance between parental rights and a child's natural right to minimal care and freedom from abuse continues even today. But at least we are beginning to acknowledge that parents do not have absolute life and death authority over their children. There are limits.

We must never allow adults to destroy the children they have a right to correct. Nor can we allow them to maim, cripple, or handicap children they have a right to discipline. Children are people too, deserving of the basic respect due all human life. The Judeo-Christian belief in human dignity has no age limit.

Theoretically, children in our modern society possess the same basic rights and protections as adults, clearly provided by the 14th Amendment to the Constitution of the United States. But in reality, this is merely the ideal. And as we all know, the ideal and the real are often worlds apart. In actual practice, children often are denied their natural rights, both at home and in society, because of their inability to demand them, and because they are underage and cannot vote.

When I speak of "child rights," I am not referring to political or economic rights. I am talking about the right of all children to be clothed, housed, and fed until they are old enough to care for themselves; the right of equal protection under the law so that their minds, bodies, and sexuality will not be exploited or abused; the right to medical care and an education; and the right to a safe and secure childhood.

The welfare of society depends on the welfare of its children. Abused children tend to evolve into abusive adults. By stopping the plague in our own generation, we will be protecting future generations from the horror, agony, and often crippling effects of child abuse. Every child has a natural right to such protection.

Points to Ponder

1. Do we learn how to be parents by watching our parents raise us? If so, what are we teaching our children about parenting?

133

2. Are there some things about the way I raise my children that I hope they will change when they become parents? What are they?
3. Is it true that punishment usually stirs up anger, resentment, and a desire for revenge? Is this the response I want when I punish my children?
4. Are there any patterns of interaction between me and my children that do nothing but hurt? Things I say or do?
5. Do my children have rights? If so, what are they? Am I willing to surrender some of my control in order to protect their rights?
6. Am I as concerned about my responsibilities as a parent as I am about protecting my rights? What are my responsibilities?
7. Do I really have a right to raise my children as I see fit?

CHAPTER EIGHT

Myth 7: *This Hurts Me More Than It Hurts You!*

During the foster-home period of my life, I was returned to live with my natural mother three times. For reasons unknown to me, all three attempts ended with my return to foster care. As always before, I blamed myself for the failures. Something was wrong with me that made it impossible for my mother to keep me.

The grief of losing a mother even once in a lifetime can be devastating. But the cumulative effect of unresolved grief when a child loses a mother four times between the ages of five and ten can be emotionally crippling. Not only was I mentally scarred by the experience, but I developed an emotional handicap that continues to plague me even as an adult.

As my world was shattered continually by a seemingly endless series of hardships, something else happened that only recently has become apparent to myself and others. As my heart fought to survive the emotional trauma, my mind was struggling to comprehend it. Searching blindly for answers that would bring understanding, I stumbled upon the issue of justice.

135

Fair play was something I understood. Everybody should be treated equally. The rules are the same for everyone. But the more I experienced the painful effects of adult problems, the more I became aware that some people are treated differently from others.

I began to notice little things that made no sense to me at the time. Why was it, I wondered, that some children always seemed to be in trouble, while others never seemed to get into trouble at all? Why was it that some children seemed always to be chosen last, while others seemed always to be first? And why was it that adults seemed to like some children better than others?

Some children, I noticed, did not seem to be as important as others. Why? What was the difference? Was it because some children were good and others bad?

Unfortunately, that is the conclusion that came to me in my search for answers. I concluded that I was being treated differently because I was bad. When other children were mistreated, it was because they too were bad. What other possible explanation could there be?

But one day that notion was challenged by an incident that occurred at school. I was confronted by a gross injustice that set up what appeared to be an irresolvable conflict between what I *felt* to be true and what I *thought* to be true. This conflict between heart and mind lasted long into adulthood and is the root of my commitment to work for the prevention of child abuse as a child advocate. What my heart could accept as deserved punishment, my mind could not accept as fair and just treatment.

It happened during one of those times when I was returned to my biological mother. It was 1958. I was eight years old. Already I had lived in several foster homes and attended several different schools. I was glad to be back

136

with my mother and vowed that never again would I be taken from her.

But already the situation was becoming worse. I would stand with my mother and brothers for what seemed like hours in a long line, waiting to receive a box of government-surplus food commodities—butter, powdered milk, beans, macaroni, cheese, flour. But it was always worth the wait to see how happy that box of food items made my mother. Sometimes she would laugh and sing merrily as she carried the box on our long walk back to the public housing project that was our home.

For a while it would seem that my mother might be happy again. How I wished that for her! I would have done anything to keep her laughing and smiling. It was the most wonderful feeling in the world to see my mother happy.

But it would not last long. Soon the smiles would give way to that same awful worried look that seemed so much a part of her features now. Then would come the fatigue, soon followed by depression that buried her in lifelessness. Smothered in hopelessness, our family would plod methodically through one endless day after another.

Those few times when feeling would return to our numb hearts and minds were joyous times to treasure. I celebrated their coming and dreaded their going—but always prized them as my most valuable possessions.

Fall finally arrived that year and brought with it my first day at school as a third-grader. My mother came quietly into the room where my brothers and I shared a bed and carefully awakened only me.

What an incredible joy it was to see her beautiful face smiling at me! And to hear her voice calling me gently into a new day. Many mornings during the previous three years, I had waked up alone in strange places, with strange faces. Though most of the people who provided me a foster home during those years were kind and generous, there was something deeply satisfying about waking up in my own bed with my own mother nearby.

My breakfast that morning consisted of one slice of white bread dipped in bacon grease. There was not much else in the house to eat. Carefully, my mother put two slices of the bread into a small paper bag for my lunch.

Going to school by myself was scary—the building was so big and there were so many other students. I felt lost and very alone. But somehow I managed to find my way to the right classroom.

The morning passed quickly. I walked around the playground alone during the lunch recess, wishing I was at home with my mother. Most of the other children were involved in games or swinging or playing chase. But one boy seemed to be as alone as I was.

He was sitting on a bench near the fence. I could tell he was unhappy. But I could not tell why.

After a while the boy got up and started across the playground toward a group of other boys who were choosing sides for kickball. It was then I noticed that the boy walked with a severe limp. He reminded me of a child I had known in one of the foster homes. He had had polio. This boy's speech was slurred as he asked if he could play.

I watched as he stood there with the other boys, waiting for someone to pick him for a team. But he was never picked. After all the other boys had raced off to start the game, the boy sat down on the school steps and watched.

I could understand why no one would pick a boy who could not run very fast, but something deep inside my

138

mind began to question why the boy could not play if he really wanted to. It did not seem fair that he could not play simply because he could not run as fast as the others. Nor did it seem right that neither team captain would pick him. The more I thought about it, the more I was sure the boy had been wronged. A flicker of anger stirred in me.

That is the first time I can remember feeling anger on behalf of someone else. It was a new and strange feeling. I did not know what to do with it. Always before, my anger had been directed either at myself or at a playmate, but always in defense of myself. Now I was feeling angry because someone else had been mistreated!

Although I did not know it then, that anger would be fueled through the years by injustice and eventually would be turned upon the injustice itself. That same anger now rages within me as an unwavering determination to cry out, stand up, speak out on behalf of those who cannot defend themselves against abuse!

Soon the bell rang and recess was over. It was time to line up near the steps and march in single file back to the classroom. The boy with the limp was already sitting on the steps, so he was first in line. But the herd of boys who had been playing kickball came running up, jostling among themselves to see who was going to be first, and the boy with the limp was knocked down in the scuffle. Picking himself up, he made his way awkwardly to the boy who had claimed his place as first in line. When that boy refused to move, the boy with the limp grabbed him by the arm and tried to pull him out of line.

At that moment the school door opened and the teacher

stepped out. When she asked what caused the scuffle, several of the boys shouted that the boy with the limp was trying to break into the line.

I listened in shock as the teacher believed what she heard and made no effort to ask the boy if it were true. Instead, she reprimanded him loudly in front of the entire class. Then she raised a ruler, which she held firmly, and told the boy to hold out his left hand, palm up.

"This is going to hurt me worse than it will you!" she said sternly. "But you must be punished. No hitting is allowed in this school!"

Five times she hit his open palm hard with that ruler. The boy stood there, not daring to move, tears streaming down his face. After it was over, the teacher made him go to the rear of the line.

I hurt for the boy. I knew all too well what it was like to have people do things to you that you did not deserve. I wished there was something I could do for the boy. But the one thing I could have done that might have made a difference, I did not do.

Many times in the years since, I have remembered that boy and the injustice done to him. I have also remembered just as often that I knew the truth and did not speak up!

To this day I do not know why. Maybe it was my fear of challenging authority. Or maybe it was because I was afraid of getting in trouble myself. Or maybe I feared the crowd of boys would turn on me.

For whatever reason, I remained mute, and an innocent boy was punished for something he did not do. He suffered alone and in silence, just as I would suffer alone, in the silence of those around me, during the days and years ahead. I would wonder then, as that boy surely wondered, why no one cared enough to help me.

I returned home from school that day to find a state child-welfare car parked at the curb. That could mean only one thing.

"This hurts me more than it hurts you." The social worker spoke softly as she led me from the house to the car. She carried a small bag of my clothing under one arm. "But I have no choice. I have a nice foster family waiting to meet you."

Unintentional Hurts

There were times when it seemed that during my whole childhood I was being hurt by people who were trying not to hurt me. Always, they were trying to help. And always, whatever they did was for my own good.

I have no doubt that the social workers had my best interests in mind as they moved me from home to home during my six years in the foster-care system. I am even sure that my adoptive parents had my ultimate welfare at heart in the beginning of our relationship. They did not adopt me to abuse me. Like most abusive parents, they were not malevolent people. I am also sure that the police officers who kept picking me up off the street as a runaway cared about what happened to me, as did the probation officers, the counselors, schoolteachers, church workers, and other people who moved in and out of my life during that time. I do not believe any of those people wanted to see me being hurt and abused. And certainly no one wanted to hurt me more in their attempt to help. But that is what often happened.

The infliction of pain to relieve pain is a common practice in the medical profession. A physician will give a shot, for example, in the hope of preventing a serious

141

illness. The ethical justification for that practice is based on the belief that in all things, we must strive for the greater good or the lesser evil. A shot is less damaging than a life-threatening illness. Clearly, giving the shot is the less painful option.

In most cases involving medical treatment, the ends justify the means—that is, the prevention of a serious illness justifies administering a less painful treatment. *But never does the medical profession ignore or deny the pain caused by the treatment.* It is acknowledged as an unavoidable side effect, and every effort is made to relieve discomfort. *And never is the infliction of pain the goal of medical intervention.* It is always a by-product. The most compelling injunction of the Hippocratic Oath is this: *First, do no harm!*

No such oath is required of parents. And yet parents are medical, psychological, educational, religious, social practitioners, who have a dramatic impact on the lives of their children. Not a day goes by that parents do not need to apply their knowledge and skills in each of these areas. How many parents even recognize, let alone acknowledge and attempt to relieve, the pain they inflict upon their children as they apply remedies to childhood problems?

Whenever we intervene in the lives of others, whether children or adults, "for their own good" or against their will, we inflict some measure of pain. Always, we must measure the pain we inflict against the pain we relieve. If, in our attempt to help we inflict more pain than we relieve, then we must seriously question the helpfulness of our intervention.

In parenting, as in all helping professions, the ends do not always justify the means. Sometimes the way we go about trying to solve a problem is more damaging to a child than the problem itself! The teacher who hit the boy to prevent him from hitting other children certainly did more harm than good.

Parents must be forever sensitive to the possible pain they inadvertently inflict upon their children. Particularly dangerous is our carelessness about what we do and say, and our unwillingness to recognize the possible harm we may have done. The greatest obstacle to positive change in families whose children suffer from abuse and neglect is the denial that a problem even exists. Until a problem is acknowledged, treatment is impossible.

Another serious obstacle that must be overcome is the rationalization we use to justify what we are doing. In most child abuse cases, parents claim a religious reason for their actions. The second most common rationalization is that it is for the child's own good. This becomes more credible when we attach the element of personal sacrifice: "This hurts me more than it hurts you!" How can we possibly give much attention to the hurting child when the parents profess their own pain so loudly?

Every action results in a reaction. Generally, positive actions by parents result in positive reactions in children. Negative or punishing actions result in harmful reactions. The same is true in adult relationships: The best way to get a smile is to give one; similarly, one of the quickest ways to start a fight is to throw a punch!

Parental Intentions

Besides the fact that the teacher used the very behavior she was punishing as her way to control the child, what was most disturbing to me was not the physical pain of the ruler on the boy's hand—that was bad enough—but his

143

mental and emotional suffering. He already felt different from the other children, and then was publicly humiliated in front of the entire class. Imagine the embarrassment! Not to mention the fact that the teacher made no effort to hear his side of the story. She assumed his guilt without question.

I have no doubt that her basic intentions were good. She may have been using physical punishment in an effort to control what she perceived to be an antisocial tendency, which, if not corrected, could cause the boy serious problems later. It is also likely that she was attempting to retain control of her class in order to maintain an environment conducive to learning.

There is nothing abusive about correcting a child. Nor is there anything abusive about wanting to maintain order in the classroom. The "what" the teacher was trying to do and the "why" she was doing it are not in question. It is the "how" that is questionable. Was it really necessary to hit the child in order to accomplish the goal? Was there not a disciplinary technique available that would not carry with it the risk of suffering? Did it really have to hurt to be effective? Could she not have used *discipline* more effectively than punishment? Why not take the two boys aside privately to discuss the matter? Or use a technique directly related to the offense? People who hit people in our society generally are disciplined by loss of the freedom to associate with people for a while.

In my own childhood, I do not doubt for a second that the people who tried to help me meant well. Nor is there any doubt that the immediate goal of intervention on my behalf was successful. That goal was to provide a home, and they did that. Again and again. But when judged by long-term effects and consequences, their intervention was a dismal therapeutic failure.

144

Short-term gains must be measured against long-term losses. If, in the end, children lose more than they gain in our attempt to help, then we must reevaluate the effectiveness of our efforts on their behalf.

We have mentioned that it is not the parents' intention to be abusive in most cases of child abuse in its early stages. It is the methods they use to achieve their goals that become abusive. This becomes clear when we consider the most common rationalization confessed by adults who sexually abuse their children. These people tend to convince themselves that they are providing sex education! They convince themselves that what they are doing is in the child's best interests, that, at the very least, the child will gain accurate information about human sexuality.

It is the parents' responsibility to provide basic sex education for their children. It is an important part of every child's education, and a part we dare not overlook. The consequences of ignorance in matters involving human sexuality can be catastrophic, as witnessed in the shocking statistics involving venereal disease and adolescent pregnancy. There is nothing abusive about giving children sex education. But having sex with them is not the way to do it! Good intentions must result in good actions or the intentions are meaningless.

Parenting Goals

The establishment of goals is the first step toward achieving them. It does not matter what we do if we have no reason for doing it, and most parents do not have specific developmental goals for their children. Such goals as wanting children to "be happy," or "become successful," or "be good people," or "get an education," are so

145

generalized they are practically useless when it comes to successful parenting.

The more specific the goal, the more specific the actions required to achieve it. Successful parents tend to know what it is they are trying to achieve. As a result, they plan and implement parenting strategies specifically designed to achieve that goal.

Quieting a crying child, for example, can be achieved in a number of ways, each having different side effects on the developing child. The child could be held and cuddled, or rocked, or distracted, or spanked, or threatened, or we might seek the cause of the distress.

Which of the many methods available we will use depends largely upon what we are trying to achieve. If our primary goal is to keep the child quiet, we are more likely to use a method that will accomplish the goal quickly, such as threatening a spanking. On the other hand, if our primary goal is to discover what is causing the child to cry—so that we can correct it and eliminate the need to cry—our approach will be quite different. The identification of the problem often will suggest its own solution.

Either approach is likely to have some degree of success. The first approach (rocking, distracting, or threatening) treats the symptom (the crying) but tolerates the cause and only tends to aggravate the problem. The second approach treats the cause, solves the problem, and eliminates the symptom. In either case we have accomplished the goal. But in which case is the child better off because of our intervention?

Identification of clear and specific goals is the first step toward becoming an effective parent. The second step is to learn effective ways of achieving those goals.

Assertive and Passive Parenting

Most of us do not act until there is a problem. This is true of our parenting as well as in our personal lives. Our parenting tends to be a constant stream of reaction and adjustment to the constantly changing problems and demands of our children. We do not forecast future difficulties but wait passively until they are upon us, and then make a desperate scramble to try to overcome them.

I have seen this dynamic of denial at work hundreds of times in couples I have worked with in marriage counseling. Most problems in marriage usually began months, perhaps even years before, but went unnoticed, unacknowledged, and untreated. One of the great American myths and greatest hazards to any relationship is the notion that if we ignore it, it will go away. Couples wait until the marriage is bankrupt before they seek help, and many times it is too late. This is like waiting until you have been fired to find out what you are doing wrong on the job.

Similarly, many parents are reluctant to deal with problems in the family while they are still mild and manageable. Rarely do these problems solve themselves. Instead, they tend to get worse, until finally there is a crisis that must be dealt with. But by this time the problem is much more complex, the remedy no longer so simple, and the effect on family members more severe.

Most of us would not wait until our car stops running to take it to a mechanic. We would not wait until we are near death to seek medical attention for an illness. The cost of such delays could be devastating. And yet when it comes to family or parenting problems, the potential loss is just as great, but we wait until we are on the verge of physical, emotional, or spiritual disaster before we act.

147

Unable to immediately discern the nature of a child's problem, for example, parents may dismiss it as a phase the child will outgrow; they may regard this period of family life as a time to "get through." Rather than persisting to discover the source of the problem, they may react to disturbing symptoms by punishing the child. That is like bringing in a fan to blow away the smoke while making no effort to locate the fire!

Many family relationships suffer from severe neglect and deprivation; they are starved for attention, care, and affection. We attempt to live and grow in a wasteland of human emotions where only the strong survive. And we wonder why we are in trouble?

If only we would treat our relationships as we do our automobiles! Regular checkups and maintenance visits are essential to keep a car running, just as checkups and regular reviews are important in parenting relationships.

But even more important is the need for parents to initiate activity designed to *prevent* problems! The best treatment for child abuse is prevention, and the same is true for alcoholism, domestic violence, smoking, chemical addictions, teenage pregnancy, academic failure, and most other serious social problems.

Such an approach to parenting is called *primary prevention.* Just as eating a proper diet can prevent the onset of certain illnesses, effective parenting can prevent certain social, emotional, and spiritual ills. Assertive parents act *before* the problem occurs, in an effort to *prevent* it. Assertive parents are effective parents.

Consider, for example, the issue of lying. Most of my childhood was lived in a world of deceit and illusion, a world where reality was dictated by the whims of controlling parents, and nothing was more true than the madness around me.

I know now that truth is the foundation of life, of reality, of mental health. Any life without it, or any relationship not rooted in it is destined to self-destruct. Truth is real. We can believe it, build on it, trust it.

I want to believe my children, no matter what they tell me, and realizing the temptations of childhood, I knew the day would come when they would be tempted to lie. Most children lie to avoid punishment, criticism, or loss of love and acceptance. They are so desperate to please their parents that they dare not admit to being human and making mistakes. They will deny a mistake even occurred; they will hide it from themselves as well as their parents, so as not to risk their disappointment and bring on the punishment.

I began primary prevention when my children were still very young. First, I assured them again and again that there was nothing they could possibly do that would be so bad that I would ever hit them. I did not mean I would never become angry or upset and discipline them. I meant only that I would not hit them.

Second, I began to tell them that I was sure they would never lie to me; no matter what they did or how bad they thought it might be, I knew I could trust them to tell the truth. They heard me say this a thousand times during the early years of their lives.

As my children grew older, not once did I punish them for telling the truth. In every instance, praise was always the first part of any discipline I used. The next part of that discipline, then, was to deal with their problem or mistake in a way designed not to punish, but to avoid a repetition of the error.

149

By substituting discipline for punishment, my children were freed of fear so that they could tell the truth. They did not need to fear the consequences. To breed honesty, we must take the punishment out of being honest.

By encouraging them to tell the truth during their formative years, repeatedly expressing my belief that they would never tell a lie, guess what happens when they are tempted to lie today? At that critical moment of decision, what do they hear echoing in their subconscience? Do they hear a critical parent, accusing them of being a liar? Or warning them against what will happen if they lie? Or the echo of other times when they were punished after being honest? No. What they hear is the voice of a loving, caring father who believes in them and knows—not thinks, but knows—they will not lie!

The emotional discomfort they would feel by violating my trust is far greater than any possible punishment I might administer. They would rather assume responsibility for their thoughts and actions than take the risk of destroying my faith in them.

Whereas the goal of punishment is to control, the goal of discipline is to teach children to control themselves. The first step in becoming self-disciplined is to assume responsibility for one's own thoughts, feelings, and actions. Everybody makes mistakes. My children know I will not be disappointed when they make mistakes. Nor will they be punished.

They also know that most mistakes can be corrected. In our family, discipline is used when mistakes occur; there is no criticism or punishment. The person who has made the mistake assumes responsibility for it, repairs any damage done, and learns how to avoid similar instances. The goal

150

of discipline is to learn from mistakes so that they will not be repeated.

I was an effective parent in this instance because I knew that the temptation to lie would eventually come, and I began to prepare for it long before it arrived. If I had adopted the attitude of "We'll deal with that problem when it comes," I would have been a passive parent, naively waiting for the problem to rear its ugly head.

The most serious effect of passive parenting is that by the time a problem does surface, both parent and child are likely to be extremely limited in terms of knowledge, skills, and resources available to deal with it. In addition, it requires a great deal more attention, effort, and sacrifice later than if the problem had been prevented in the first place. In such situations, the parent usually punishes the symptom while ignoring the problem, which grows worse over the years until it becomes a major crisis in the life of an adolescent.

To say that an ounce of prevention is worth a pound of cure is an understatement.

The Challenge of Child Advocacy

I did not speak up on behalf of the boy at school that day so long ago. And no one spoke up for me during all those awful years. But no longer will I remain mute to the truth! No longer will I sit silently by while children are being abused.

The truth is that it hurts a great deal *more* to be hit than to hit, to be abused than to abuse. I will speak up, cry out, and shout the truth, until at last the screams of our children are heard above the roar of those who would profess an even greater hurt than the pain they inflict in the name of love—or madness.

151

Points to Ponder

1. In my attempt to be a good parent, do I occasionally inflict unintentional hurts upon my children?
2. When I discipline my children, do I sometimes wonder if I am hurting them more than helping them? When were some of those times?
3. As a parent, do I tend to treat symptoms, or causes? Do I punish unwanted behavior because I do not like it? Or do I seek the cause of the behavior and try to correct it?
4. Do I sometimes rationalize that what I have done or said to my children is for their own good? Or that I had no choice?
5. Do I somtimes punish my children with the same behavior I am punishing them for? Do I scream at them not to scream at me? Or hit them for hitting?
6. Do I have parenting goals? What are they? Are they specific and attainable?
7. Have I developed parenting strategies for achieving those goals?
8. Am I an assertive parent, or a passive parent? What is the difference? Am I sometimes assertive, sometimes passive? How does this affect the health and development of my children?

CHAPTER NINE

Myth 8: *Spare the Rod and Spoil the Child!*

There is reason to believe that our image of hell comes from a place where children were burned alive as sacrifices to the pagan god Molech.

The Valley of Gei-Hinnom is a deep ravine running south from Jerusalem's Potsherd Gate. A procession of people would leave the city through that gate and move down the valley to a place called Tophet, which means *firepit,* near where the Valley of Gei-Hinnom intersects the Kidron Valley.

Parents would bring their newborn children to the god's sanctuary in that valley. The people would gather and, in ritual celebration, lay the infants on the outstretched metal arms of the god and watch as they tumbled helplessly into the fiery furnace at this feet.

The books of Kings, Chronicles, and Jeremiah in the Bible repeatedly mention this sacrifice of children. Out of that madness and the suffering it caused, arose the classical description of hell as a place of eternal pain and suffering.

Infant sacrifice was popular during the golden age of

Solomon and under the reigns of Ahaz and Manasseh, who are recorded as having sacrificed their own children in this manner (II Chron. 28:3, 33:6). The prophet Jeremiah foretold that during the Last Days, the Valley of Gei-Hinnom would be called Valley of Slaughter, an abomination in the sight of the God of Israel (7:32, 19:6).

During the reform of Josiah, the sanctuary of Molech was converted into a garbage dump that was kept burning day and night (II Kings 23:10). Over the years, the concept of hell evolved into a place of despair, darkness, and death for the condemned; a place of stench, filth, pain, torment, and misery.

A derivative of Gei-Hinnom, the word *gehenna* came into use during the century before the birth of Christ. It was used to describe a place of fiery torment—the lake of fire—believed to be reserved for the wicked, either immediately after death or after the Last Judgment.

The Contemporary Parallel

Isn't it ironic that the classical description of a fiery hell also accurately describes the home environments of many American children? For most severely abused children, their home is a crucible of torment from which there is no escape. Those who are able to survive can never completely erase the memories that haunt their lives. It is a painful and tragic truth that even today, children continue to be sacrificed to the gods of ignorance, tradition, and human madness.

Although condemned by lawmakers, the practice of infant sacrifice continues as a painful social reality. Children are no longer taken in large numbers to the

Valley of Gei-Hinnom, but they continue to be sacrificed nonetheless, one by lonely one, in their own homes, where they should be safe from all danger.

The reasons for the maltreatment of children are many and varied. But whether to placate the furies of mind and body or simply to be rid of an unwanted child, the effect remains the same: Helpless children are crippled and destroyed.

Though the names and places have changed over the millennia, the reality of hell in the lives of countless children has not. There exists no greater hell than that experienced by the thousands of severely abused children who continue to fill our cemeteries or, when grown, our prisons and mental institutions.

Throughout history, childhood has been a dangerous time of life, and it remains so even today. Infanticide, torture, physical and mental cruelty, abandonment, incest—all are extreme forms of child abuse which continue to be documented daily.

Righteous Violence

Child abuse is an incredibly complex problem, once it has occurred. How it can happen, in what otherwise appear to be healthy families, remains a mystery to most of us. Yet the reality is undeniable.

Although many dynamics in the abuse cycle have been identified—dynamics which set parents up to abuse and their children to be abused—never will there be a completely satisfactory explanation for violence and abuse in the family. Child abuse is an irrational act that arises out of forces astir in the dark side of our nature, which compel us to do evil instead of good. That dark side is unpredictable and inexplicable, and has no master apart from the evil it serves.

Although we have much to learn, we do know that almost all cases of physical child abuse have at least one thing in common: The parents believe it is acceptable for an adult to hit a child—as long as there is no *intent* to harm the child; hitting is done as an expression of love, for the *benefit of the child.* Actually, most child abuse is the result of ignorance and tradition.

I stress these points because of their importance. Child abuse is made possible by virtue of the human capacity both to deny reality and to rationalize it. Like all evil, child abuse is perpetuated when its existence is denied. And its continued presence is assured when its use is justified by the rationalization that it will achieve some good purpose, or that it is an expression of love.

Beliefs Behind Parenting

Too many parents are willing to do just about anything to their children if they believe it is a good and desirable thing or that it is God's will.

Despite the pain hitting might cause, or the long- or short-term consequences, many parents believe there is no other way, and that it is their responsibility to use any means necessary to control their children. They believe their success as parents will be measured in terms of control, and how they achieve this goal is unimportant so long as it is achieved.

Some parents even believe it is their Christian duty to administer physical punishment—to build character, discourage sin, and instill a sense of submission and obedience to the will of God, as represented through

156

parental authority. They take what God has created in his own image and refashion it so their children will grow up to be just like them! They think they must tame children as they would domesticate wild horses, so they will quietly take their places in society—a society that must serve the will of the masses as expressed through those few.

Almost invariably, abusive parents will justify their actions on righteous grounds. They most often appeal to a higher principle, such as religious duty or love of their child. Their attitude is that anything is acceptable as long as it is done in love. My adoptive parents told me hundreds of times, during the endless beatings, that they loved me. If that was their way to love, they very nearly loved me to death!

Despite all the rationalizations, of course, most acts of violence directed at children are not done with the best interests of the child in mind. Nor are they expressions of love. More often, they are expressions of pent-up frustration and anger, a means to meet the needs of the adult: A parent may use violence to control a child in order to regain a sense of control over some difficult situation.

Righteous violence is violence used for a presumed righteous purpose, so that its inherently evil nature is overlooked. We use an evil to achieve a good. War is a classic example. We kill people in defense of ourselves and our country. Self-defense is a justifiable use of violence, but that does not change the evil nature of violence. Where we make our mistake is that we do not confess and repent the evil we have done as we celebrate the good we have achieved. The result is that we are still more inclined to use violence to fulfill our wants, needs, and desires.

Capital punishment is another classic example of evil

used to achieve a good. We kill people who have killed so that the killing will end. To stop the killing is good. But is killing to stop killing less evil than killing for personal profit? Yet most of us support capital punishment; we do not acknowledge it as inherently evil—despite the commandment that so clearly tells us it is forbidden! That is righteous violence.

When Judas led the soldiers to the Garden of Gethsemane, one of the apostles attempted to defend Jesus with his sword. Our Lord immediately repaired the damage to the ear of the slave of the high priest.

Then Jesus said to the apostle, "Put your sword back into its place; for all who take the sword will perish by the sword" (Matt. 26:52).

Three days later, Jesus had been beaten by those who condoned the use of violence against prisoners; then he was crucified by those who condoned the use of capital punishment to exact justice.

And while still in the midst of his pain and agony, our Lord said, "Father, forgive them; for they know not what they do" (Luke 23:34). He forgave them the evil they did as they fulfilled the demands of Roman justice. Not only did our Lord refuse to use violence to save himself, he forgave the ignorance of those who cost him his life!

Righteous violence claimed the life of our Lord, and it has taken the lives of thousands since. It continues to be used to justify violence within the family, especially that which occurs between parent and child.

Violence by choice will inevitably become violence by chance. Those who practice it by choice will surely suffer when they encounter it by chance on the street. As long as we condone the use of violence and allow it a place in our lives and relationships, we shall continue to be threatened

158

by it, our lives will be controlled by fear, and our capacity for hope, faith, and love will be diminished!

Is Spanking Children Our Christian Duty?

I recently attended the meeting of a government committee reviewing the use of corporal punishment with institutionalized children twelve years old and older. The consensus of those state agencies charged with the care of abused and neglected children was that the practice of corporal punishment should be eliminated because it was ineffective, in many cases counterproductive, and in the long run did more harm than good. They concluded that hitting children may control a behavioral symptom, but rarely does it resolve the cause of the problem. The control of symptoms is not the goal of state intervention on behalf of abused children. The goal is, and must continue to be, the resolution of the problem.

I was there to speak out in support of legislation to eliminate the use of corporal punishment. My only regret is that the proposed legislation did not offer the same protection to all children, regardless of age, sex, or circumstance. But at least it was a step in the right direction!

As the meeting began, several impassioned Christians stood before the committee, each waving a Bible in one hand while clenching the other fist, declaring it to be God's absolute will that "children be subjected to the rod of correction." Quoting passages from Proverbs, they announced their duty as Christians to "spank" the children placed in their care—but only in "love" and always for the child's own good.

In dismay, I listened as they preached the same righteous violence that cost our Lord his life. Professing to

159

be his followers and teach his will, these people were advocating, in the name of Jesus, for all to hear, the willingness to use violence against children as a necessary quality of all Christian parents.

I wondered then, as I continue to wonder, if Mary and Joseph used violence against Jesus during his childhood. Although there is little written about that period of his life, we do gain a glimpse of their relationship when we read of the journey to the temple when Jesus was twelve years old. As you recall, his parents started home unaware that Jesus had remained behind in the temple. They traveled three days before they discovered him missing. Returning to the temple after being separated from their son for six days, they found him pursuing his education with the temple priests, apparently unconcerned about their worries. Nowhere is it written that Mary and Joseph went into a rage and spanked Jesus for the distress he surely caused them. What parent would not have been so tempted?

I also wonder how many of those good Christians invite Jesus into the room when they spank a child? I cannot imagine Jesus ever hitting a child! In fact, he told us it would be better for those who make a child stumble if they would drown themselves in the river.

There is no doubt in my mind that those people know well the power of prayer. I am also sure that most of them practice it routinely. Surely they pray before meals and before retiring for bed. And surely they pray before making momentous, life-changing decisions. But how many, I wonder, pray before they spank a child?

There is also no doubt in my mind that those people believe what they were saying to be true. They are well-intentioned. But so were the astronomers who, for centuries, convinced us that the sun revolves around the earth and that the earth is flat. The physicians who practiced bloodletting—the use of leeches—were every bit as sincere and convinced of the value of what they were doing. The same can be said for the good people of Salem who sought to be rid of the evil presence of witches, or the parents who swaddled their children immediately after birth, or those who drowned their children born with handicaps because they were not created in the perfect image of God, or the good Christians who continue to believe that God is an Anglo-Saxon!

The social and religious history of the human race is a testimony not only to its advancement of knowledge and incredible achievements, but to its ignorance. In all knowledge there exists a degree of ignorance because we can never know it all. For every truth there is a greater revelation, a deeper understanding; truth is constantly unfolding. And those who claim to possess it are those most likely to deny it when they encounter it standing before them.

Streams of Religious Teaching

The people who testified before the committee firmly believe it is God's will that they spank children, and their reasons can be understood more easily if we review two main streams of religious teaching.

Both streams of thought represent the extremes along a continuum, and although American parents lean toward one or the other, most of us fall somewhere between the two. The two perspectives are well woven into the moral and ethical fabric of our culture, and the one we tend to believe will have a profound impact upon the way we raise our children. Both openly religious and nonreligious parents are influenced by these teachings—some more than others.

161

The first school of thought teaches that a child's basic nature is evil because of "original sin," and the Fall of man and woman in the garden of Eden. By rebelling against God, disobeying his order not to eat fruit from the tree of life, Adam and Eve were forever cast out of the garden. They became subject to death, slaves to their sin, and would spend the rest of their earthly lives struggling to overcome the rebelliousness of their basic human nature in order to reclaim eternal life.

Children are born with this same basic evil nature, this perspective teaches, and to allow this nature to continue would be to jeopardize their hope for eternal life. It is likely that children who rebel against parental authority will also rebel against God's authority; whereas the first may jeopardize their life on earth, the latter could well jeopardize their heavenly life.

Therefore, the goal of all Christian parents is to save the souls of their children from eternal damnation. To do this, the parents must transform that basic evil nature into a nature that is good and acceptable in the eyes of man and God. They must break the evil spirit of rebellion and teach the children to be submissive to the will of God by forcing submission to parental will. Disobedience is punished to teach children obedience to the will of God, since eternal life comes only to those who obey his Commandments.

The human body, from this perspective, tends to be viewed as the prison of the soul, a source of constant weakness and temptation that encourages sin. Therefore the body must be kept pure and its influence upon the soul kept within controllable limits through the purifying effect of pain and sacrifice. Physical punishment thereby builds character, discourages the ways of the flesh, and

162

inspires the soul to seek the rewards of eternal life rather than those of the earthly life.

Since the basic nature of children is evil and the human body merely a prison of the soul, it is, then, the parents' God-given duty to use any means necessary to save the souls of their children. In most cases this means they must literally "beat the devil" out of them!

The other stream of teaching, quite the opposite of the first, teaches that the basic nature of all human life, especially that of children, is not evil, but tends toward goodness. Children are created in the image of God, and God is certainly good; therefore children created in that image must possess the same basic qualities. This belief is reinforced by the Genesis story of creation: After God created man and woman, he pronounced them not only good, but *very* good!

If children are already basically good, a parent's duty is to nurture the spirit so it will flourish into that which is God's will for it. The goal of parenting, then, is not to change children, to transform them from evil to good, but to make them more of what they already are—inherently good.

The human body, from this perspective, is not a prison of the soul, but the temple of the spirit! When being challenged by the religious authorities of his day, Jesus referred to his own body as a temple that would be raised again in three days. We would never treat the walls of a temple as we might treat the walls of a prison, would we?

Instead of beating the devil out of children in order to break their rebellious spirits and thereby save their souls, the call to parenting from this perspective is a call to stewardship. We are shepherds placed in charge of God's own sheep—his children. It is our duty to nurture the

163

spirit, not break it; to protect the body, not strike it; to be good stewards of what God has placed in our care.

Differing Parenting Practices

There are profound differences, not only in perception but in the practice of parenting, between the people who believe those opposing teachings:

1. Obviously, those who believe that the basic nature of children is evil will be more inclined to use harsh, physically punitive methods of *punishment*. Those who believe their basic nature is good will be more inclined to use positive methods of *discipline*.

2. The first type of parent is likely to perceive childhood instances of misbehavior as *crimes* deserving of punishment, whereas the second group is likely to perceive them as *mistakes* that need discipline.

3. Instead of *punishing* children for being human—for being what they are by nature, as in the first teaching—those who believe children are created in the image of God *reward* them for being human—for being what they are by nature.

4. Parents who believe children are inherently evil take a negative approach: They seek out flaws and weaknesses in order to correct them. The other parents do not look for what is *wrong* with their children, but notice what is *right*. Their goal is not so much to correct and change as to praise and nurture. These parents tend to see children as the precious miracles they are, reflecting the beauty and goodness of the Creator, rather than the worthless creatures they could be, reflecting the ugliness and evil nature of the Destroyer.

5. The relationship of parent and child in the first

instance is rooted in the power of parents to control children. It is based on *fear, pain,* and *intimidation.* The relationship of parent and child in the second instance is rooted in the sanctity of all human life. It is based on *love, trust,* and *mutual respect.*

6. The basic goal of the first group is to *control* their children. The goal of the second group is to *teach* children to control themselves.

7. The first group is at a much higher risk of *abusing* their children, whereas the second group is at a higher risk of *spoiling* them.

8. Those who believe the basic nature of children is evil are more likely to use an *autocratic* parenting style that involves a double standard: They tend to adopt a "Do as I say, not as I do!" style. Those who believe the basic nature of human life is good are more likely to use a style of parenting that involves *modeling:* They teach by example, practice what they preach.

Like the three servants placed in charge of their master's talents, the day will come when we must give an accounting of our stewardship as parents. It is then that the sheep will be separated from the goats, those who walk in the ways of Jesus from those who walk in the ways of Barabbas.

Punishment Versus Discipline

There is a vast difference between discipline and punishment. Yet most American parents confuse the two or think they are identical. Often we punish when our intention is to discipline.

As we have seen, the goal of discipline is to teach children to control themselves, while punishment pursues

165

revenge, exacts retribution, controls. Teaching is of little concern during punishment.

Discipline is best taught by example, by parents who model self-discipline and acceptable behavior. Punishment is imposed and is most effective when administered by a more powerful adult, whom the child can neither intimidate nor escape.

Discipline always builds children up. They feel good when they are able to see their mistakes and correct them. Punishment not only inflicts pain but always instills a sense of guilt for not being "good" enough. It inspires children to deny mistakes for fear of punishment.

Discipline acknowledges the difference between children and their behavior. It recognizes that there is nothing "wrong" with children, that their basic nature is good; it is the *behavior* that is unacceptable or inappropriate. Children have some control over their behavior, whereas they have none over their basic nature!

Punishment suggests that there is no difference between children and their behavior. It is the child who is bad or unacceptable, and as a result, it is the child who is punished, not the behavior. The tragedy is that the only possible response children can have to punishment is the feeling of guilt and shame for being who and what they are, since they can do nothing to change their basic nature.

Discipline perceives childhood misbehavior as a mistake that provides a learning opportunity. Punishment perceives that misbehavior as a crime that deserves punishment.

Discipline is a way of life practiced by all members of the family. Punishment results from a double standard and applies only to children.

Discipline strengthens character, enhances the ability

166

to discern right from wrong, and rewards efforts at self-discipline. Punishment weakens character, erodes self-confidence, damages self-image, and instills fear as a primary emotion between parent and child.

Spanking: Discipline or Punishment?

The debate about whether spanking is discipline or punishment has raged for centuries and continues today. Its proponents argue that it teaches the unpleasant consequences of certain behavior and thereby serves as a deterrent to repeated misbehavior. To the extent that it teaches children to control themselves, it is discipline, they say.

There can be no doubt that spanking can "work." Pain is an incredibly effective motivator. Violence gives immediate short-term control. And this is what most parents want when they are looking for something that "works."

But hitting teaches children some very important lessons about human relationships. It teaches that some hitting is acceptable—but not all hitting. It teaches that it is OK for big people to hit little people—but it is not OK for little people to hit back. It also teaches a definition of parental love: Parents who love their children hit them!

Many hidden problems inherent in spanking can have a serious impact upon the lives of children, their families, and society in general. There are as many definitions of spanking as there are people who do it. Parents tend to define *spanking* by their own experience. If what they are doing falls within the range of their own childhood experience, then—regardless of its severity or effect upon the child—it is not child abuse. It is only a spanking. To this day, if my adoptive parents ever make any reference to

167

the beatings they inflicted upon me, they invariably call them spankings!

I was trying to make this point on a television talk show one time when a young mother called in.

She said, "I have just spanked my three-year-old daughter. She has a welt on her bottom that is bleeding. Is that child abuse?"

The woman was serious! She really did not know whether hitting a child so hard it left a bleeding welt was a spanking or child abuse.

"If your husband put a welt on your bottom that was bleeding," I answered, "would you call that spouse abuse?"

There was no hesitation in her answer. "Well, of course!"

"Then why do you need to ask if it is child abuse? A child's bottom is made of the same flesh and blood as that of an adult. It hurts just as much. Why should age be the criteria for determining who will be hit and who will not be hit?"

The more hitting occurs in a family, the more it will be tolerated and overlooked. A slap on the wrist can evolve into several slaps and then into a slap on the bottom, then several swats on the bottom, then into a belt, a paddle, or a switch, perhaps even a closed fist.

Those who use violence with their children are the very people who may have the greatest difficulty controlling it. The parent must believe it is acceptable and a good thing, but studies clearly show that the most common type of physical child abuse is the "spanking that went too far," or the result of "losing control."

Chronically abusive parents tend to have low levels of empathy. They have difficulty in vicariously experiencing the pain and suffering they are inflicting upon their

168

children. Yet this is the very dynamic that inhibits aggression in every healthy personality. Without empathy, parents are likely to inflict far more upon their children than was their original intention.

A parallel can be drawn between child abuse and alcoholism. Both, at this point in our history, are legal. Yet it is acknowledged that both can cripple and destroy.

Alcoholism begins with the first drink. Child abuse, with the first blow. Both are most treatable after the first blow (or drink) and become progressively less treatable. If left untreated long enough, the cycle of both may reach the point of chronic denial, at which time effective treatment is unlikely until there is a "bottoming out" experience. Prior to that point, there is still hope for successful intervention. But hope grows a little more dim with each blow (or drink), the chance of rehabilitation less, and the chance of permanent tragedy more. Both must be caught early in the cycle if treatment is to be effective.

This means we must deal with child abuse while it is still a "spanking," before it becomes a beating. But how can we treat it at this point, when so many people believe spanking a necessary function of every parent.

Not all parents who spank will cripple, destroy, or damage their children, just as not all those who drink will become alcoholics and kill us on the highway, or rape, rob, or murder us under the influence. But alcoholism is a serious problem. And so is child abuse. It is the foremost killer of children under the age of three in this country!

Violence is like a drug: The more it is used, the more it takes to achieve the same effect. It can become habitual. It can become a master we serve as it slowly destroys us!

The issue is not so much whether spanking is right or wrong. The issue is more practical. Few of us would tell an

169

alcoholic it is OK to drink socially. Yet, how many of you would tell me it is OK for me to "spank" my children? Like an alcoholic who dares not touch liquor, I dare not use violence with my children. To tell abusive or potentially abusive parents it is acceptable for them to "spank" their children is setting them up to be abusive. In essence, it is a license to hurt.

Many of us do not care to acknowledge that most spankings occur not because children's behavior is bad, or inappropriate, or disruptive, or destructive, or defiant, or rebellious, or any of the many reasons parents cite as justification. If the truth be known, most spankings are administered when a parent is angry, tired, or frustrated and a child's behavior is distracting or perhaps merely inconvenient.

Reasons for Opposing Corporal Punishment

Why do I say corporal punishment should be abandoned as an acceptable parenting tool?

1. It is unnecessary. There are nonviolent disciplinary alternatives which are even more effective and pose no risk of harm to children.

2. It confuses discipline with punishment. Discipline is used to teach, while punishment is used for purposes of control and retribution. Young children do not commit crimes that require a punishment reaction. Their mistakes call for a corrective disciplinary response.

3. It validates fear, pain, intimidation, and violence as acceptable methods of resolving conflicts between adults and children.

4. It preempts better means of communication and

problem solving. As long as it is an available option, little effort will be made to learn nonviolent alternatives.

5. It confuses the issue of love and violence, teaching that violence can be an expression of love. True love is expressed in much healthier ways.

6. In that all human behavior is symptomatic, it merely controls the symptom while aggravating the cause of the personality disturbance in the child.

7. It is dangerous, in that it can escalate into battering.

8. It increases aggressiveness in the child and vandalism in the school and on the street. Violence perpetuates violence.

9. It can result in permanent physical, mental, spiritual, or emotional harm to the child.

10. It reduces the ability of the child to concentrate on intellectual tasks and thus inhibits learning.

11. It denies the child a right to equal protection under the law—a right guaranteed to all natural-born citizens of this country in Section 1 of the 14th Amendment to the Constitution of the United States.

12. It violates the standards of judicious discipline, based on Judeo-Christian ethics and the principles of child rearing.

The United States is one of only a few civilized nations in the world that still practices the systematic spanking of children. Such notable groups as the American Medical Association, American Bar Association, National Parent Teachers Association, National Mental Health Association, N.A.A.C.P., and the National Committee for the Prevention of Child Abuse have taken stands opposing the use of corporal punishment in our schools and homes.

171

Force has no place where there is need of skill.

—Herodotus

Spare the Rod and Spoil the Child

We have seeen that many parents justify the use of corporal punishment first as their righteous duty in response to the will of God, and then as their responsibility to society to raise well-disciplined children. Quoting the passage from Proverbs in the Bible—"Spare the rod and spoil the child"—many parents believe Scripture encourages, even prescribes the use of violence as good and necessary. Few of these parents will acknowledge, however, though it has been proved again and again, that it is possible to raise healthy, well-adjusted children without once hitting them.

All things are a gift from God. Whether a cup, a pen, a car, love, money, trees, or children—all are gifts from God. All these gifts have an equal potential for good or evil. Which of the two will be manifested depends first upon how we perceive it, and second, upon how we put it to use.

I can perceive this pen in my hand as an instrument of communication and use it to write a book on child abuse. That is good. On the other hand, I could perceive this same pen as a weapon and use it to put out someone's eye. That is evil. It is the same pen but it has two opposite uses—one good and one evil—depending upon how I perceive it and how I put it to use.

The same is true for a rod. It too is a gift from God. It too can be used for good or evil, depending upon how we perceive it and how we use it. A rod does not need to be used to beat, torture, and destroy. A rod can be used, instead, to guide, steer, and protect.

The "spare the rod and spoil the child" passage from Proverbs is a call to *discipline*—not punishment. It is the rod

172

that brings comfort, as in the Twenty-third Psalm: "His rod and his staff, they comfort me."

There is no place in healthy Christian families for violence. Regardless of what we may call it, violence is violence, whether directed at a child or an adult. It is inherently evil and in direct conflict with the love and peace prescribed for us by our Lord. Jesus told us to love one another as he loved us. Surely this includes our children!

The effects of violence are similar for all victims. They hurt. A lot. Sometimes for a lifetime!

Points to Ponder

1. Is it possible to raise children without hitting them? Is it possible to raise children without spoiling them?
2. If so, why don't we? What do we have to lose?
3. Do I believe it is my Christian duty to "spank" my children? Is it God's will that I physically punish them?
4. Are children born inherently good, or are they inherently evil?
5. Is the human body a prison of the soul, or is it a temple of the spirit?
6. Can I do *anything* to my children as long as I believe it is God's will? Can I do anything to my spouse for the same reason?
7. Does "spare the rod and spoil the child" mean I should physically punish my children, or that I should discipline them?
8. As a parent, do I look for what is wrong with my children, or for what is right? Is my primary function to nurture them, or to correct them?
9. Would Jesus ever hit a child?

173

CHAPTER TEN

New Hope for Lost Childhoods

By the time I was seventeen, I had survived almost seven years of severe physical and emotional, as well as sexual abuse. It was clear by then that the only way to survive was to kill my parents before they killed me. Everything else had failed. Hiding had not saved me. Trying to be what they wanted me to be had not saved me. Telling someone outside the family had not saved me. Nor had running away. Nothing had worked. I could see no option.

I was a survivor. Survivors will do whatever is necessary to survive, so I began to make plans.

I will never forget the last beating I received at their hands. Always before I had cowered like a terrified animal. But not this time! I was so filled with bitterness and hatred and the desire to kill that I no longer cared what they did. I did not move, did not cry, did not show any reaction at all. After seven years of beatings and torture, I was filled with a homicidal rage.

That was the night they kicked me out of the house and told me never to return. It was a good thing they did, because I probably would have tried to kill them. Had I tried and succeeded, society would have finished the process of my destruction.

That was twenty years ago. By that time I was a very angry young man, with the self-esteem of a worm. Despite all my parents had done, the person I hated most was myself. People did not beat and abuse me because they wanted to, I believed, but because they had to! I was bad, a low-life who did not deserve to be loved or wanted. People don't love trash; they kick it, smash it, and then throw it away.

Today I am a reasonably well-adjusted husband and the father of three children. I live in a middle-class neighborhood, where several neighbors seem to like me. No one here fears me. I attend church regularly and am active in its ministry. No one seems to fear me there, either. I attend all my children's ballgames and other special events. The people there seem to feel safe enough around me. I have a doctorate from a prestigious university and make my living as an educator in the field of child-abuse prevention through ICARE (International Child Advocacy and Resource Enterprises), the nonprofit ministry I founded in 1983. I have written four books to date, two of which are Angel Award winners, and am under contract for a fifth book.

The question I am most often asked—How in the world did you survive, Phil? And survive so well?—is one I continually ask myself. Most people who have experienced childhoods such as mine have self-destructed. They usually end up in prison, a mental institution, or a graveyard. How did I make it when so many do not?

New Hope

In most areas of life it is impossible to regain that which is lost. How often we are reminded that we cannot turn back the clock! What is past is gone. What remains is memory.

While it may be true that we cannot physically relive yesterday, there are times when the past remains very much alive and well within us—times when what was is just as real now as then. Who has not felt the sharp pain of grief as vividly, remembering the death of a loved one long ago? How many of us have memories of early life events that stir feelings similar to those we felt when the event occurred?

Adult personalities are largely the result of childhood experiences. Most emotional problems stem from an unpleasant experience never forgotten.

Childhood has a ripple effect throughout our adult life. Although our bodies may grow, and we may mature and be forced to think and act like an adult, the child within us lives on. A happy, well-adjusted childhood filled with pleasant memories tends to result in a similar adulthood. The opposite is also true. Rarely do happy adults grow out of unhappy childhoods. It does not matter how big, or how strong, or how old we become, the child within us continues to live.

For some of us, an unhappy childhood leaves scars which permanently set us apart from other people. For others, they are only blemishes on our personality, which may irritate from time to time but have no serious or lasting effect. Still others carry the result of our childhood as disfigurements or handicaps which inevitably affect our posture and walk through life.

Those whose childhood was damaged by suffering and misery must find other things upon which to build their adult lives—forces external and perhaps alien to their own experience. For some, it is the expectations of other people; winning the approval of others becomes a life obsession.

176

For others it is material success, professional accomplishment, or any of the myriad psychological mechanisms that can be employed to deny the past in hope of preserving the present. But whatever the case, each of these people continues to experience the result of a lost childhood.

But there is hope. Although we can never relive our childhood, we can certainly reexperience it. It is the experiences of childhood, more than the events themselves, that have shaped us into what we are today. And it is the experience, not the event, that must be relived in order to reclaim a lost childhood.

I have survived better than most because I have rebuilt the foundation of my life. My perception of reality—my thoughts, my beliefs, my behavior—all have changed. I have replaced lies, deceit, and illusions with truth. The hopelessness that trapped me in despair has been replaced with a boundless hope—a faith that makes all things possible. The bitterness and hatred have been turned upon the evil that is its cause. Like a serpent that swallows itself, the evil is being consumed by the very forces it created.

A flood in a valley is welcome irrigation in a desert. The rage that so overpowered others and threatened my own destruction is now channeled into a welcomed ministry of reconstruction—the rebuilding of shattered lives. Empowered by a Spirit not my own, I have been shown *the way* to unlock the prison of my childhood.

Reclaiming Lost Childhoods

Many years are required to find the way and learn how to use the key. It is a process of healing, growing—a pilgrimage out of darkness into light—which I began in 1975 when I first admitted I was a victim.

177

1. *Admit to being a victim.* Unhealthy childhoods are usually ignored or forgotten. The adult often finds it better to pretend that such an unfortunate time never existed. This is called *denial.* For years I denied, to myself and to others, both that I had been abused and the effect that abuse was having on my life. I continued to tell myself that I deserved what my parents did because I was bad; they did it because they loved me. As long as I lived that lie, I remained a slave to it. Not until I could really believe I did not deserve it, did I begin to reclaim my lost childhood—and thus the rest of my life.

2. *Be honest about what really happened.* It was not enough to admit I was a victim. Just as important, I had to be honest about what really happened. I became much healthier when I stopped using the words my parents used to describe what they did—spanking, paddling, whipping. When I could at last call them *beatings*, I took a giant step toward conquering my past.

3. *Acknowledge the problems it has caused.* Problems cannot be solved unless they are confronted. There is no weakness, no shame in admitting problems. It was not until I could admit to myself that I had a problem with intimacy, with trusting, with loving, with parenting, and with sharing myself that I took the first step toward resolving those problems. This required a level of personal honesty that at first appeared brutal. But I soon learned that brutality exists only in deceit. In honesty, there is only redemption. What is not honest is not real, but an illusion. And it is not possible to build on an illusion; sooner or later the illusion will come crashing down. Honesty is real. It can be trusted. However painful, a relationship, or a life, *can* be built upon it.

4. *Tell someone else.* After coming to grips with the

reality of my abuse, I needed to find some way to express the feelings it stirred in me. I first began to do this by putting them on paper. But that was not enough, because I could not trust my own judgment about what had happened and why. My tendency was to blame myself, to assume responsibility—and to deny consequences. I needed to tell someone—someone I could trust, someone who could reflect with me about the experiences in a way that would not judge or deny them, but perhaps would bring enlightenment. Therapeutic relationships in which I could talk, and cry, and scream, and rage were particularly helpful in diffusing the incredibly powerful emotions that had seemed such a part of me. Talking out the abuse, though it may take years, is very important.

5. *Learn about it.* The more I was able to identify the problems and their effects on me, the more I needed to understand as much as possible about child abuse and domestic violence. I read every book, every article, every report I could find on the subject of child abuse. The more I read, the more I realized that what happened to me happens to thousands of children, and it is not their fault. This study of child abuse helped to bring some order, some understanding to the madness of my experiences. It helped rationally explain what had happened and later supplied the clinical background I needed to be able to assist other victims.

6. *Accept the limps.* Desperately, I had wanted to be like other children, to have a family that loved and wanted me. I wanted a happy childhood, filled with memories to treasure. I wanted a mother. But now I had to accept that none of these would ever be mine; I would have to live without them. Nor would I ever be "normal" in the sense of being unscarred. The abuse had damaged me perma-

179

nently. The scars would be with me throughout life. I had to accept that, too, and even more, I had to understand what that meant in relation to the rest of my life. The abuse had left me with physical, mental, emotional, and spiritual limps. But just because I am physically damaged does not mean I cannot function. I just function with a limp. I think with a limp. I feel with a limp. I believe with a limp. But limps need not stop me. Instead, they can remind me of the suffering of other children and thereby motivate me to continue my work to end that suffering.

7. *Be human; allow feeling.* The more I studied and talked about the abuse, the more intense became my feelings. I found myself openly and unashamedly wanting to hate my adoptive parents, to hurt them as they had hurt me. This was a difficult but significant step forward, in that, for the first time, it put the responsibility where it rightfully belonged.

As I stopped blaming myself and the world around me, an amazing thing began to happen: My depression began to lift. Slowly, the burden I had carried through most of my childhood began to lighten. In time, my attitude and behavior began to change for the better. All my feelings were now directed at my parents.

This step is particularly hard for those raised in religious environments, where hate is seen as a sin. But the only way I could ever hope to love passionately was to hate passionately until the hate was gone. When I allowed myself to be human, to feel what anyone would feel under similar circumstances, without guilt or shame, I began to accept myself. This was important, because eventually I could stop abusing myself as my parents had done. It is not unusual for victims to perpetuate their victimization into their adult lives, picking up where their abusers left off.

180

8. *Reexperience childhood.* As I began to talk and write about the abuse, I allowed myself to reexperience what I was describing. One of my greatest fears was that if I ever mentally relived those abusive incidents, I would surely lose my mind. I had survived them once. I was not so sure I could survive a second time.

I discovered, though, that now I could reexperience them as an adult, with knowledge and understanding, and certainly with some sense of personal power. I was not the helpless child who could do nothing to stop what was happening, but an adult, who could redefine the experience for what it really was and put the responsibility where it truly belonged.

Reassessing childhood—renaming, relabeling, redefining, and reinterpreting abusive experiences—is an important step toward accepting them as something that cannot be changed or ignored, but which need not control the rest of one's life.

9. *Take charge.* When I experienced for the first time a deep compassion for the child I had been, with a better understanding of what had happened, filled with hope for a new tomorrow and rage at the injustice, I vowed to be a victim no longer. I made a conscious decision to take charge of my life. Like a farmer tending the fields, I would decide what would be planted in my life and what would be cast out. No longer would I live to please others. No longer would I run from the past, hide for fear of being found unworthy, or try to escape unwanted memories. I could do nothing to change what had occurred. But I could control today and tomorrow. And I chose to exercise that control. At that point, the important shift occurred: I was no longer controlled by the past, but by the future.

10. *Help someone else.* Sometimes the wounded are the

181

best healers. Once I began *doing something* about my own life, I found myself wanting to do something for others who had suffered as I had, and to do something about child abuse. Slowly I began to reach beyond my own problems, my own wounds, to touch the wounds of others. And an amazing thing began to happen. I discovered that whenever I reach out to touch another person, I am always touched in the process!

My own grief and suffering lessened as I worked to lessen the hurts of others. I learned that out of the madness that was my childhood came something important that I could share with others: myself—a former victim, someone who has been there. Having stared evil in the face, how much easier it is to recognize goodness! Because I have known so much ugliness, how much more I treasure the beauty that exists in all things!

11. *Allow the child to live.* The world is never a more beautiful place than when seen by the eyes of a child. Love is never more real than when felt in the heart of a child. Life is never more joyful than when experienced as a child. The child within me still existed. I had to let him live! I had to unlock the prison doors and allow the child within me to feel, to care, to love again. I had to laugh and cry with him! Sing and dance with him! And allow the child within me to meet the children around me. I began taking extra time, making an extra effort to understand the problems, concerns, and joys of the children I saw. I began trying to protect them from what I had not been protected from. I allowed myself to feel and think like a child.

12. *Release the past.* Once a man was working at the top of a high tower. He did not notice the storm approaching until a bolt of lightning struck the tower somewhere below him. The shock caused one of the tower's legs to buckle,

and it leaned precariously to one side. Then a fire started at the base of the tower.

The man could barely hold on, but he knew that if he fell he would surely be killed. But he also knew that in minutes the tower would be engulfed in flames. He was trapped!

Realizing there was nothing he could do to save himself, the man prayed that God might deliver him from the death that surely awaited him. No sooner had the words left his mouth than an angel appeared, suspended in air just beyond reach.

"Have you come to save me?" the man asked anxiously.

"Do you believe the Father sent me to save you?" asked the angel.

"Yes, I believe God has sent you!" answered the man eagerly, and he waited for the angel to grab him.

But the angel did not move.

Desperately, the man cried out again. "Aren't you going to save me?"

"If you believe the Father sent me to save you, do you also believe that I will do as the Father commanded?" asked the angel.

"Yes! Yes, I believe you will save me!" the man answered as he watched anxiously for some move from the angel.

As before, the angel did not move, but seemed to be waiting for something. Panic-stricken now, the man could barely hold on.

"What must I do to be saved?" he screamed as his hands began to slip.

After another moment of waiting patiently, the angel spoke. "If you truly believe the Father sent me to save you, and you truly believe I will save you, then why don't you let go?"

I had to let go of the past. Release it. It was a stone

183

around my neck. I wanted to be free to live today and tomorrow without fear and guilt. But like so many victims, I waited and prayed and begged God to heal me. Like the man on the tower, I waited for God to make the first move. It was some time before I realized that healing requires a leap of faith, a letting go that requires absolute trust in God. I had to act on my faith. I acted; God responded. And I was saved!

13. *Unlock the prison of childhood.* Although I had come far in my pilgrimage toward freedom, there was still something missing. I had not yet quite arrived. Deep within my heart I still carried bitterness, hatred, a desire for revenge. I knew these feelings would rob me of the rest of my life if they were allowed to remain. Such feelings are weeds which, if allowed to grow, will strangle all the good things that might have grown. Like weeds, they must be plucked out and left behind. There is no place for such feelings in a healthy adulthood.

What was missing was forgiveness. I never really had forgiven my parents. And though I never may be able to forget the acts of atrocity, I had to forgive the persons behind the acts. So I began to look for someone to teach me how to forgive.

I did not need to look far. I was reading the Bible one day, when for some reason, I was drawn to the crucifixion passage. I read about how Jesus was denied and betrayed by the very people he loved most. Then he was arrested, tried, and found guilty by the people he had come to save. They insisted that he be executed, though the state was willing to set him free. While in custody, he was physically and emotionally abused, and he was made to carry his own cross to the hill upon which he would be hanged. Then he was crucified.

I was there as I read. I watched and listened from the crowd. How many times had I betrayed and denied him in my own life? How many times had I yelled for the execution of another human being? How many times had I physically and emotionally abused someone? Jesus had said that whatever I did to the least of those, I did also to him.

What physical and emotional agony he must have felt. What incredible hurt! And yet, even in the midst of suffering, he begged God to forgive the people he still loved, for they did not know what it was they were doing.

The power of that single act had meant very little to me until then. But suddenly, it meant the whole world. Jesus forgave the people because of their ignorance. He forgave me! For I was there also, standing in the crowd. His eyes rested upon me as surely as they had rested upon the others.

Was it possible that my parents really had not known what it was they were doing? Was it possible that they had been as ignorant as those who screamed "Crucify him!"? Or as ignorant as I? Suddenly, I believed so.

And out of that belief came my ability to forgive. In forgiving my parents, not only was I resurrected into a new life, free of the horrors of my childhood, but my childhood itself was redeemed. Out of that suffering has come a life commitment to work for the prevention of child abuse. *Forgiveness* was the key to unlock the prison of my childhood!

Preventing Child Abuse

The prevention of child abuse—stopping it before it occurs—requires a shift in attitude and thinking by most

American adults, as well as by lawmakers. This shift must occur in several important areas:

1. *Parents do not own their children.* We must accept and believe the fact that parents do not own their children as legal possessions. There is a minimal standard of care and nurturing that must be provided, regardless of age, beyond which parents are free to raise children as they please. But they do not have absolute, unquestioned authority. There are limits to what parents and caregivers can do to and with their children.

The right to parent carries with it the responsibility to parent within acceptable social and legal limits. To exceed those limits is to forfeit that right, and thus state intervention is required on behalf of the child.

2. *Every child is the rightful concern of every adult.* Most of us believe we are responsible only for the care of our own biological or adopted children. We often ignore the needs of children not our own, trusting that someone else or an agency will tend to their special needs. In so doing, we implicitly condone and encourage abuse.

In order to prevent child abuse, we must begin to understand that adult responsibility toward children does not end with our own, but extends to all children everywhere—the kid next door, down the street, along the highway. In a sense, all children are our children, deserving of our time, care, and attention.

As members of the human race, we have the responsibility to care for those of our own who are incapable of caring for themselves. To deny or deprive even one helpless child of food, clothing, shelter or other basic human needs is a crime against humanity, for which we all should and must be held accountable. Given the wealth and resources of this nation and others, there is no excuse for even one child anywhere to lack the basic life necessities.

3. *Acknowledge the basic human rights of all persons.* Equal protection under the law is a right guaranteed all citizens of the United States, regardless of race, creed, sex, or age. Children have more right not to be hit than parents have to hit. Children have more right to the privacy of their bodies and minds than parents have to invade or violate those minds and bodies. And certainly, children have a right to a safe and healthy childhood, free of abuse and exploitation.

4. *Change our approach to the problem.* To date, most efforts to focus attention on child abuse have been attempts to determine, in specific instances, whether someone has done something "wrong" or "bad" to a child. Our attitude has been judgmental and punitive, looking at behavior in terms of whether a parent should be punished or whether the state should intervene. Such a negative, self-defeating approach has resulted far too often not only in greater harm to a child and eventual breakup of a family, but also in waves of public panic that have a frightening resemblance to a Salem witch hunt.

If we are to prevent child abuse, our attitude must change. Rather than trying to determine what parents are doing wrong, we must focus our attention and concern on whether they are doing what is necessary for the child to grow and develop normally, within the family's unique environment. Rather than seeking out parental "crimes" against the children, we must turn our attention to deficiencies in the parent-child relationship which can be corrected for the benefit of the family, enabling the adults to become better parents. Our goal is to help, not hurt; to build and strengthen, not weaken and destroy.

187

I am calling for a more positive, constructive approach to parenting and its problems—an approach that will strengthen the relationship with support and education rather than weaken it with threats, accusations, labels, and unnecessary punishment. Abusing a family while protecting one of its members from abuse is not the answer and can only perpetuate the problem.

5. *Accept a preventive definition of abuse.* A legal definition of child abuse has as its purpose the setting of legal restraints, within which the state can and must intervene in instances of abuse, and the setting of guidelines for doing so. A preventive definition has as its primary purpose the prevention of child abuse in the first place. To that end, it is not punitive or accusatory or judgmental. Instead, it describes and prescribes a standard of parent/child interaction which involves mutual respect and appreciation for the sanctity of all human life, with the intent of providing a healthy environment for the entire family.

Such a standard of interaction acknowledges that certain behaviors result in pain and suffering and should be avoided. It also recognizes that the means parents employ to achieve certain goals with their children are as important as the goals themselves.

There is no greater threat to individual and public peace and welfare than that posed by physical and emotional violence. It is everywhere around us, rumbling almost unnoticed through the personal encounters of our daily lives. And it is learned and perpetuated by ignorance and neglect.

If we are only as good as we feel, then it becomes imperative that we do all in our power to help our children feel good—not only about themselves, but about the world in which they live. Only by controlling violence will we find solutions to the ever-present problems that pose such an ominous threat to the continued existence of humanity as we know it. Ultimately, this means we must bring peace to our children, both yours and mine. Peace to our families. Peace to ourselves. We must stop hitting.

EPILOGUE

Our Challenge

There is a valley in Israel that runs from the Mediterranean inland to the Jordan River. It links northern and southern Palestine and in biblical times was called the Plain of Esdraelon. This valley has been an important military and trade route throughout history. Those who controlled the valley controlled most of Galilee, as well as the important land routes. As a result, many battles were fought over it.

Midway between the Mediterranean Sea and the Jordan River, two cities were situated opposite each other along the valley. One city sat atop a hill on the north crest of the valley, while the other topped a hill on the south.

The city to the south was called Megiddo. During much of its history, Megiddo was occupied by warlike peoples who swept down out of the walled city to raid and plunder the trade caravans which passed through the valley on their way to Syria and Mesopotamia. The people were violent and brutal, leaving death and destruction in their wake. Today the city of Megiddo lies in ruins.

The city opposite Megiddo across the valley is Nazareth.

The home of Mary and Joseph, it was in this city that Jesus grew up. Throughout history Nazareth has been peaceful, occupied mostly by craftsmen and farmers. Today this city is alive and thriving.

It is not only time and history that separates these cities, nor is it a way of life that preserved one and destroyed the other. They are separated by the valley.

The Plain of Esdraelon is also called the Valley of Jezreel. Here, we are told, between living Nazareth on one side and dead Megiddo on the other, the Battle of Armageddon will be fought.

Armageddon is to be the final battle between good and evil. Satan will fight with the evil spirits of deceit, violence, and death, pouring out from the ruins of Megiddo; God will fight with words of truth, peace, and love—the words of the Messiah, who came from Nazareth. In that battle good will triumph over evil, and Satan will be destroyed forever.

Whether the Battle of Armageddon actually occurs on the location designated for it, or merely in the hearts of human beings, it will occur. Preparation for it has already begun and continues each day of our lives. Everywhere we turn, the forces of good and evil are opposed in love and hate, war and peace, right and wrong.

The day will surely arrive when all of us must stand up and declare our choice. Like the people so long ago who were asked to choose between Barabbas and Jesus, we too are asked to make a choice. To choose Barabbas is to choose the way of violence, suffering, and death; that road leads to Megiddo.

Whether we arrive in Nazareth or Megiddo will be determined by the step we take today. One step along the

191

path of violence will inevitably lead to a second and a third, until we have traveled so far that we are lost.

Whom do you choose—Barabbas or Jesus? How will you live—in love and peace, or in violence and suffering? Does the path you walk lead to Nazareth, or to Megiddo?

Choose Jesus. Choose to walk in his ways, to live as he lived. There is no place in healthy families for violence of any kind, for any reason. Join me and all the members of ICARE in our crusade to end the reign of terror. Help us stop the hitting.

ICARE (International Child Advocacy and Resource Enterprises) is a growing movement of caring people who have made a personal commitment to prevent family violence and child abuse. Established in 1983, ICARE is a nonprofit organization founded on the belief that the best solution to family violence and child abuse is to prevent it—to stop it before it starts.

Violence will continue to threaten us as long as we ignore its presence and allow it to flourish where there should be only peace. The way to escape the madness is to deny it a place in our hearts, in our lives, and in our homes. Let us find reasons to hug, not hit!

ICARE

P. O. Box 499
Hermitage, Tennessee 37076